Daniel O'Leary was born in 1961 in Hampstead, London. *The Loss of a Mother* is the first in a trilogy of stories and is his first novel. Almost anything and everything else about him is contained within the three works.

DANIEL O'LEARY

_____

THE LOSS OF A MOTHER

A TRUE STORY

Contents

The Slap

A Dangerous Ambition

The First Letter

The Interview

The Second Letter

The End of the First Chapter

———————————

THE LOUNGE

He believed that it all began the fifth time that day that his father got up from his chair and walked over to his supine, near comatose and bed ridden wife and placed his hand on her breast to feel for a heart beat. The boy was sitting reading some comic book or illustrated history of the Saxons or some other such publication and raised his eyes almost desultorily to watch his dad execute his layman's examination. Michelle, his sister was sitting almost opposite, but on the other side of the bed, equally occupied in her own childish and limitless world of imaginings and narrative that probably spoke of journeys through the clouds, lofty love ambitions and tales of hope without obstacle. He took in the picture with a strangely surreal comprehension given his tender seven years and youthful perception. The bed where lay recumbent his dying mother, although he could not remember later if he understood then that she was dying, the bed which could be a sofa too, was the focal point of the living room. Centred by three armchairs in almost triangular dimensions, his father had been sitting in the middle of the three, flanked at some two meters or so either side by the boy and the girl, engrossed in their respective literary outlets. With retrospect, how bizarre a scene it must have appeared, three people, one adult and two children, were busily and quietly digesting frivolous script whilst a fourth person, an adult, lay busily and quietly dying.

At the time he believed that it all began there, but actually it had truly begun two years earlier, on a balmy summers day in 1966, a year punctuated with knighted world cup winners, a world class boxer refusing to take his fighting skills to war, moving rocks providing musical notation for a tin of black paint and his mother being diagnosed with a brain tumour. That requires clarification. Her brain tumour was *diagnosed* but she was not the recipient of those tidings. Medical prudence at that time suggested another course of revelation which did not always involve the patient knowing at all. This at least was what he heard later but had always been sceptical that she wasn't aware and this scepticism was not founded on some nebulous platform of arbitrary guesswork so much as observable reality, especially one mid morning in autumn 1967. He believed it was autumn but the passing of time tends to occlude the precision of memory. Suffice to say, the day was cloudy although this may have been the mood rather than a realistic appraisal of the season. His father, his mother and himself, they were all three in the lounge, the lounge in the first floor flat in Belsize Park that served as both lounge and parents' bedroom, his father was about to leave, striding down Cressy Road, towards the tube station and the underground to work, work that involved shifts that saw him toil at varying hours wherein he spent his time distributing tickets to travellers wending their way back and forth to their own place of travail, fulfilling the Myth of Sisyphus with relentless repetition. It was middle shift and the hour neared eleven. He lent down and kissed his son goodbye and leaned over to kiss his wife too and then turned on his heel and left.

Danny's mother walked to the window overlooking the street and observed her husband pacing away. He sidled up beside her, raising the net curtain as he did so and pressed his face hard against the cold and clammy glass noticing how his breath passed invisible onto the pane and all at once lost its cloak of unseenness as it created random patterns before him. With a smile of unmitigated and innocent pleasure, so particular to the purity of children who discern wonder in most anything, he looked up to his mother to seek her unspoken response. To his mild dismay, she was not watching him but had her eyes firmly on the back and hairless head of his departing father with tears carving minor rivulets on one cheek.

'Mummy, what is the matter?' he asked as he took her hand tightly in his own. 'Why are you crying, Mummy?' She didn't answer, just squeezed his hand with intended re-assurance and with her free arm, reached in her pocket for a tissue to remove any evidence of distress. Little Danny was the only witness to this event but even then, he was sure his mother wasn't crying for the temporary absence of his father, he was sure of it.....

~~~~~~~~~~~~~~~~~~~~~~~~~

THE GIFT OF LIFE (*the first failure*)

He certainly knew it was an autumn day when his mother died. October in fact. October 1968. A Monday. He did not know the date exactly. In fact he would never know the date. Not because he couldn't have found out. It was simply that there was no point, no need, it just wasn't relevant nor important. However, he remembered the day itself because that would be the last day he ever saw the inside of Cressy Road, he remembered because that would be the last day he spoke to his mum.

It began as another morning that had assumed the demeanour of normality at that time. He was sitting on the side of that bed, the same bed that featured so heavily in the closing chapters of his mother's life. She was still comatose, drifting in and out of consciousness but clinging to life with the residual threads of the tenacity of survival, the last strand of defence against the inexorable onslaught of ultimate ruination, laying still, head turned to the right, away from where he sat. It was school time. The Rosary School. Where his friends were, his best friend, Peter Bell, *DingDong* as he was universally known, with not the least element of perjorative slight attached. It would be either Mrs Tate, the sweet, gentle Mrs Tate, a friend from nearby, or Mrs Gibbons, upstairs neighbour, stern Mrs Gibbons who would escort him and Mitch to school. A relatively short walk but one whose distance, as all distances, was magnified by the little feet of little people. Today however, that day, he wanted Mrs Gibbons to take them, not Mrs Tate.

That may seem strange when Mrs Tate was such an endearing soul but the little lad had good reason. It was because of the last words that were exchanged between himself and his mum.

He was quietly sitting on the side of the bed, swinging his leg back and forth, skirting the floor with his shoed heel, school tie askew, short grey trousers and school jumper thrown on with indifferent abandon, his mother barely aware of his, or anyone else's presence. But there was no-one else present. The only sound that periodically punctuated the silence was the gentle hum of a car engine passing in the street below seeking to cheat the early morning traffic snarl by exploiting the sleepy, little used Cressy Road. He didn't know what words could make her better. He wasn't sad, his mum was just unwell, she would get better, he was convinced. He had tried to help her get better before. It must have been winter when he had tried previously, or certainly a colder season as he was wearing an overcoat, an item that would serve as an integral component in his attempt.

He was sitting in the classroom when an idea of incomparable quality struck him. Perhaps if he got his mother a present, some gesture of tangible substance, perhaps that would aid her recovery. He had no money, so he couldn't buy anything but there was a wealth of material right before him in the nature of books, Ladybird hardback books. They would make an admirable gift and small enough to smuggle. Not one though. A whole raft thereof. He would steal some hardback Ladybird books and present them to his mother as unwrapped offerings to facilitate her return to robust and ruddy health.

He had his coat on which extended down to his bony knees, it would simply be a matter of selecting the books, no need for specific selection, the choice wasn't particularly material, hide them below his coat, and secure their position with his hands clasped together, seemingly assisting the buttons in holding the coat closed against the insistent cold striving to breach its outer barriers. The teacher always left first, leading her chattering children out of the class. He would ensure he was the last to exit the class, at the last minute turning his back momentarily to the motley file of youngsters leaving their quotidian activities to re-join the fabric of their familial lives, embraced in the grasp of loving environs and the normality of growing up. Or returning to endure the heavy, unspoken sadness that pervaded those Hampstead halls which could only be created by the relentless demise of a loving thirty-eight year old mother of two…

The moment arrived; he would later come to believe that his heart was beating heavy in his chest but that belief could well have been born from assumption rather than sure knowledge since it would seem fair to assume that any potential act of theft would be accompanied by a thudding heart and tremulous nerves. However, with a deft dexterity, the provenance of which could not be identified, the child grabbed six or seven books, who knows what number, and in the split of a second had them ensconced within the safe and secure layers of coat and hands. He then nonchalantly attached himself to the departing file, books in situ, thoughts focused on how very, very pleased would be his mother when she witnessed the beautiful gesture which he had executed so seamlessly.

His only minor concern was the walk home and the need to hold the books tight that far. Still, the concern was only minor.

They paraded untidily onto the playground leading to the gate where liberation awaited them all for another evening and twenty or so children sauntered seemingly carefree and unaware of life's less joyous facets. The gate was approaching with a drawn out and protracted arrival and all he could now think of was who would be picking him up. Mrs Tate or Mrs Gibbons. The gate was but metres away now and he was once more looking forward to the mutual delight that would be engendered when he gave his mother these books. True, they looked a little tatty, well and oft used and manifestly second hand but there was nothing that he could do about that. Besides, his mum wouldn't care. He could already feel the big, big cuddle and the hug, safe and warm as she would hold her tight to him and he would hold her tight back, on tiptoes, trying to gain her height. And the smile, he could actually *see* her smile radiating outwards, full of joy and happiness. This would make her better, he was sure of it!

He couldn't make out who was at the gate even though it was now less than two metres away but the little boy had shifted his focus with too much emphasis and intent from *what* was beneath his coat to *who* was at the gate. That was all it took. A millisecond of concentration loss. A spit in the ocean of time. The most inconsequential fraction of infinite hours that could ever be. The books tumbled out from below the garment and dropped treacherously to the leaf swept ground. Silence. Motionless stillness. He had no idea how rapidly the thoughts came but come they did. What should, what *could* he do? He could sprint away to the safety of the person who would be waiting. But would that be safe? It depended on who it was. Mrs Tate ideal, Mrs Gibbons, better to take his chances where he was. He could run back into the main body of the school. What for? No refuge to be found inside. There actually weren't that many options.

In the end he did nothing. He prayed, really honest to God prayed, that the ground would open and swallow him up. He urged the books to vanish. He felt that he was going to collapse. His peers had formed a circle with the teacher towering among them. Their eyes, his too, turned to the books, now chaotically strewn and carelessly piled in their midst, like some waiting bonfire of duplicity, some resting half opened, top ended, some forming tepee like shapes reaching up, spine arched aloft, hypnotising them all, then their eyes turned to him. He felt like he would die, no, he *hoped* that he would die. It was unspeakable. The shame. The horror of it all. Yet not one word, not one, was uttered. No-one, adult nor child said a thing. In fact, no-one *ever* mentioned it. It was actually *never* mentioned. Ever.

Years later he would realise why he was never punished, not even told off for this blatant act of larceny. The teachers would have been fully conversant with the tragedy unfolding at his home. They were cutting him some slack.

The teacher gathered herself and gathered the books and then led them all over the last few feet to the gate and their expectant custodians. He too, reached the gate and there on the left was Mrs Tate, out of eye line and consequently, oblivious to what had just transpired. And yet all he could think, the only thought in his head, as he moved towards her and his already present sister was how terribly, terribly sad it was that his mother would never receive those books. He was heartbroken.

~~~~~~~~~~~~~~~~~~~~~~

LAST WORDS

It may have all begun the day he watched his father feel his mother's heart beat for the fifth time but there was no doubting the day it all ended, and that was the Monday in October when Martha came. That was the day the love, the happiness and his mother's thirty eight year existence came to an end. Mrs Tate had taken them to school. Danny was inconsolable that it was her and not Mrs Gibbons because of the last conversation he ever had with his mother. As he swung his leg back and forth, thinking of things to say, seeking something that would make it all better, the words, the last words although he did not know then that they would be, the words appeared before him in unsubstantiated form and in a seven year old's linear process, he brought the words to life.

'Would you like a cup of tea, Mummy?' he said, gently and with a simple, untainted sincerity that would have moved even the most hardened of hearts. He watched her as she slowly, agonisingly ingested the words and rolled her head towards him, eyes closed to a crack, a small trace of saliva bedaubing the corner of her lips, and responded in a drawling and barely audible manner.

'Oh yes pleaseeee, Danny,' she murmured. She was thirsty. It was obvious. The house was in a rush. Early morning, work waiting, school to attend but he had to get his mother a cup of tea.

Years later he would realise that she would probably never have been able to drink it even had it been provided but at that moment, he needed to ensure she got her cup of tea.

He couldn't make it himself, too young, too inexpert. Mrs Tate had arrived, presumably to take them to school; that left Mrs Gibbons. Stern Mrs Gibbons. Mrs Gibbons who lived upstairs and throughout the course of his mother's illness had performed some of the perfunctory tasks that his mother was no longer capable of doing. Without any of his mother's maternal compassion however. Like the time she washed his face with a harsh flannel and even harsher application whilst simultaneously pulling his head back by the hairs themselves for more effective access. He didn't, absolutely didn't want to entrust the question nor the task to Mrs Gibbons. He just *knew* his mother wouldn't get that cup of tea. Mrs Tate, she would do it but how could a seven year old prevail upon adults to alter their plains about the delivery of two children to school.

He asked anyway and naturally it was Mrs Tate he asked. He tugged at her sleeve as she stood, scarf adorning her head, raincoat ready and primed for an October zephyr and its concomitant precipitation. She was engaged in a conversation with someone he recalled later but could not recall with whom but he later recalled whispering, or at least quietly presenting his request.

'Mrs Tate', he uttered as he tugged her sleeve, 'Mrs Tate'. She was giving him scant regard, engrossed in loftier dialogue of lofty adults. 'Mrs Tate,' he persisted, and she finally acknowledged his presence.

'Yes, Danny?' she replied.

'Mummy wants a cup of tea, Mrs Tate. Would you please make it for her and Mrs Gibbons can take us to school.'

'Oh does she?' she answered. 'Well, I'll be taking you and Michelle to school but I'll ask Mrs Gibbons to make her one.'

'Please you make it, Mrs Tate, Mrs Gibbons can take us. Please Mrs Tate.'

'Danny, don't worry, Mrs Gibbons will do it. Now go and get Michelle as we don't want to be late, there's a good boy.'

'Please you make it Mrs Tate,' he was tugging at her sleeve again, more urgently now. 'Mrs Gibbons can take us'.

'Danny, get your sister. We have to go'.

She wasn't being nasty nor unpleasantly dismissive, it was just that she didn't share his list of priorities of which there was actually only one. Somehow getting a cup of tea made for his dying mother. Or perhaps he was unable to convey the urgency of the plea with sufficient emphasis. Whichever it was, as the three people left the front door of Cressy Road for the last time that dank October Monday morning, one of them was quietly sobbing in the sure knowledge that the woman dying in the lounge on the first floor would never get that cup of tea…

~~~~~~~~~~~~~~~~~~~~~~

THE DAY MARTHA CAME

The rest of that day passed without incident. Schooldays by and large tend to pass without major incident. Especially for 5-11 year olds. It is the repetition of known habits and same behaviour that broadly comforts children growing up. The need and desire for stability, comfort from familiarity, these are the things that construct a platform for healthy emotional development in the young. The day Martha came was the day that any remaining hope for such stability was torn asunder for the young Michelle and Danny. It was the day when they were met at the school gate by Martha.

The only thing Danny had wanted to know all day was whether his mother had received that cup of tea. He would never know. New thoughts subordinated older equivalents at the sight of Aunty Martha standing by the gate of the Rosary Catholic School that chilly October afternoon. Why was she here? Where was Mrs Tate or Mrs Gibbons? As soon as they were both within earshot, Martha said that they were all going to Gerrard Road that day. Gerrard Road, where his father's mother lived, where 2 families shared a 3 storey house plus functioning basement. His father's mother and spinster sister Grace downstairs and Martha and her husband, Charlie, a man of unsung quality, and their two sons upstairs. Gerrard Road, where they occasionally visited, although not since his mother had taken up permanent residence in the bed in that Hampstead lounge. Gerrard Road, when he once had to whisper in his father's ear when Grace made them tea, he was drinking tea from quite early on, that he didn't take sugar anymore. At the tender age of 6.

Gerrard Road, that was relatively acceptable to visit but always nicer to leave, heading back for the comforting feel and atmosphere of Cressy Road, their home, the only home that they had ever known.

They walked, the three of them, towards Belsize Park. Belsize Park was and is on the northern line and is served by a lift as well as stairs for the more fit conscious. That afternoon, they took their place in the lift, Danny on the left of Martha, Michelle to the right, or perhaps it was the other way round, both clutching a Martha hand. He couldn't stop wondering why this was happening. Why were they not going home? Why couldn't they see their mother? Where was their father? He didn't like the feelings that were touching and tickling him with tendrils of unease and he certainly didn't like this very unfamiliar behaviour. Were they going home later?

These questions were levelled at Martha but in typical adult fashion, or perhaps just Martha fashion, they weren't met with anything other than lip service to fact and veracity and gleaned over with transparently false responses as though children were idiots when in fact they are simply little adults. It made no sense, no logical cogency, not even to a seven year old. Yet still they marched on as the lift allowed access to sinewy passages of grime and posters sharing space whilst promoting grit of a real nature and two cowboys who had funny sounding names for two tough gunslingers.

The not so distant rumble of the metal snakes coiling at speed through their darkened lairs, putting to flight the reticent rats who ambulated therein, reverberated around the passages with steady thundering, given voice by palpable tremors of minor earthquake proportions.

As they arrived on the platform, southbound, Morden via Bank, their red carriage pulled in and they all boarded as one. The train was relatively empty, it was still afternoon and they found seats easily and Danny looked at the train map adorning the upper part of the carriage opposite him. He counted the stops mentally; Belsize Park, Chalk Farm, Camden Town, Euston, Kings Cross and their ultimate destination, the Angel. What irony that would one day prove to be. They were heading for somewhere called the Angel…

~~~~~~~~~~~~~~~~~~~~~~~

THE JOHNNY7

It must have been pre-1968 for obvious reasons as most of that year, his mother was bed-ridden. But it was definitely around the time of the budgie incident. He couldn't remember the name of that budgie He was fairly sure it was Cookie but he couldn't be positive. Does it matter if budgerigars don't have names? Do the budgerigars care? Cookie is as good a name as any, and better than many. His mother was certainly not bed ridden at the time of the budgerigar incident. She was vibrant and vocal and alive and subject to the fears and foibles of healthy people, people who aren't busy dying when inconsequential issues just don't matter anymore. And also, it would have been close to one of his birthdays, there hadn't been that many, at the end there would only have been seven, so it was reasonable to guess which, narrowed down all the more when taken into account is the element of memory and the ability to wield the finest weapon ever made according to him, and thousands of other boys, at that time. The Johnny7. The toy coveted by every male child and now by those adults who were once those lucky children.

He would never quite remember how it came to pass that he would even have been aware of the weapon's existence. Presumably adverts were as prominent in that era as they are ubiquitous now but of its existence, aware he was. And in that loving environment that was Cressy Road, he was atop the stairs the day he saw his father come home from one of his shifts. It was dark so perhaps middle shift, or turns as they were and are known.

Given that his birthday fell in February, when winter's dark descended to clothe Hampstead early, this would lend weight to the possibility of it being middle turn. Regardless of the precise shift, the precise timing, he espied his father enter the front door at the bottom of the stairs and attempting to conceal a long package clumsily behind his back. It was simply too unwieldy and large to disguise with a ready ease but the child, knowing instantly what the contents were, removed himself from the propinquity of the stairs so that it would not impair the surprise that his mother and father were hoping to deliver come the day of his birth recognition.

He could barely contain himself; he knew the treasure that packaging contained. It was an unrivalled mechanism. Two settings, automatic and single shot machine gun with a detachable pistol affixed to its nether regions, all green for camouflage purposes in jungle terrain (perhaps there existed a desert sand coated version although if there wasn't, there should have been) with rocket launcher and missile projectiles too. This was potentially the best present he was *ever* going to receive. DingDong hadn't got one, so an added benefit was that he would have been first among two equals, at least briefly.

His birthday arrived and his mounting excitement was barely containable. It really did feel like a living thing within him, ready to burst out in a flood of mixed entrails and viscera. The animated energy which had risen to irrepressible levels easily chased away sleep and by the time the embryonic rays of a new sun's advent seeped in through the closed curtains of his bedroom, he was exhausted with anticipation and sleep deprivation but was dismissive of the fatigue that engulfed him.

He threw back the covers, jumped out of bed, indifferent to the slumber that sought to allure him into its rigid embrace and ignoring Michelle who lay next to him sleeping with benign innocence, totally oblivious to the fact that it was only six in the morning. He raced out of their shared bedroom into that lounge where slept his mother and father. His arrival brought an end to their peaceful repose and he dashed to the side of the bed where a number of neatly wrapped shapes sat awaiting his attention whilst his parents quietly observed him.

It wasn't there. The unwieldy, large package that he had witnessed his father port through the front door was nowhere to be seen. He wondered years later if the disappointment that fell upon him like a heavy weight of unsustainable load was manifestly patent to an observer although he hoped he would have possessed the alacrity of thought and presence of mind to disguise somehow the almost unendurable despair that cloaked him in a vice like grip. He was fooling himself. His parents saw very well his sadness. They were wishing him happy birthday and lay there smiling as he began to recover and address that small pile of presents before him. He opened them all, one by one, and there were some lovely things among them, including accessories for his Action Man, his best toy from some years previously.

When he had finished unwrapping them, he clambered up onto the bed and wriggled his way in between his mother and father and popped his legs under the covers as he hugged them both and kissed them as he thanked them for the gifts and reminding his mother about the small party that awaited him later that day and to check yet again that DingDong was coming.

'Yes, Danny, for the thousandth time, he is coming,' she said, 'but don't you think you are being a little impatient?'

'I cant help it,' he replied, twiddling with her hair as he lay close to her, focused on some thread protruding from the fabric of her nightdress. 'I'm excited.'

'I didn't mean that,' she countered. 'I meant with your presents.'

'Oh, sorry'.

'Danny, I don't think you understand me, ' she continued. She had his attention now and he stopped twiddling with her hair and rolled onto his side to face her, resting his face on his elbow and looking quizzical. 'You were so busy looking at your presents, that you didn't look anywhere else.'

'What do you mean, Mummy?'

'Look over there, at the table.' He duly complied.

'But it's just a table, Mummy.'

'You are not looking hard enough,' she went on.

His face was now a picture of pure concentration and then no more; he was up and out of that bed with a rapidity that would grace a cheetah in full flow, and was at the table close to the window in a flash, tugging at what would prove to be the barrel of the weapon which was protruding out from below the table lodged on a tucked in chair, just enough to be visible from the bed.

Loosely wrapped, the paper presented no obstacle in getting to the riches below in a trice and there it was, before him, in his hands, staring up at him. A Johnny7. *His* Johnny7.

The smile that filled his face was priceless. It was a smile that would have illuminated the whole of Hampstead at the very least. He couldn't stop grinning. In fact, no-one would have *wanted* him to stop grinning, such a winning smile it was and such levels of unadulterated joy it conveyed. He ran back to the bed, weapon at the ready in one hand, with the other hugging his mother and kissing her and thanking her so much, and then his father too, and telling them both as he fled from the room,

'Love you, Mum! Love you, Dad!' as he bolted back into his bedroom calling 'Mitch, Mitch, look what I got!' and thinking how jealous DingDong would be.

~~~~~~~~~~~~~~~~~~~~~~

THE BUDGERIGAR

Why wouldn't he have been at school that day? There must have been a reason. Surely this incident couldn't have taken place before he had even *begun* school? If that were the case he must have received the Johnny7 before his fifth birthday since he had it at the time of the budgie episode and that seemed unlikely. No, more likely it was a sick day or holiday or some such.

That notwithstanding, he was lying on the floor of the kitchen which was located down four steps that led up the lounge and his and his sister's bedroom. His mother had her back to him busy at the sink and he was playing with Corgi cars, perhaps imaging himself to be driving his father's ford. The reason for his mother's presence was much more straightforward; she didn't have a job but she did work raising two children and taking care of the house and home. She also had an Avon round but that was part time and very unstructured, it simply provided some extra revenue for the coffers of Cressy Road and also to provide her with some money to treat his father to a bottle of Scotch on weekends, that one beginning with H he believed. Haig. Sometimes there was a bottle with a netting and a dimple carved into the body of the bottle itself. He liked to run his finger up and down that bottle for the ripple effect it produced.

His sister was twenty-two months older than him and so she began her schooling almost two years before he did which explained her absence.

He could only really remember spending a handful of days like that at home with just himself and his mother although in reality there would have been many, many more. Nonetheless, these memories of the time he spent alone with just his mother were some of his fondest and without question, some of his happiest. To feel unthreatened, safe, so totally loved and to reciprocate fully that love with the most important woman in his universe, these were feelings which he would miss and for which he would long throughout his life and yet which he would never be able to recover nor emulate. As they both went about their respective business that day, happy in each others taciturn company, neither could have had any idea how little time they would ultimately have together.

The budgie was in the lounge in its cage. Cookie. He did later hope it really was called Cookie. Something deep in the recesses of his memory nudged him towards this possibility, but the matter of the budgie nomenclature would remain a thing of uncertainty. Now and again, though at least once a week, his mother would let the avian creature out of its cage to fly freely in the aether as an act of kindness to an animal who would never savour the indefinable feeling of total liberation that even he himself would not finally fully taste until many years later, once the chains of suffocating control were no longer strong enough to bind a child becoming a young man.

That day was one such day wherein the budgie would be freed for its ritualistic and intermittent gyrations about the lounge.

Certain protocol had to be observed however, to ensure the process proceeded flawlessly and without issue. All windows had to be firmly shut within the lounge itself and even though the bird would be left alone inside those confines with the lounge door fully shut, nevertheless, all other accessible windows in the rest of the flat would be shut too, just in case the small creature should somehow manage to extricate its being from the larger walls of the larger prison. Once all preparations had been implemented and executed, then the door to the cage could be opened and the bird could temporarily flee its residence at its leisure. On occasion, if he was there, his mother would allow him to open the cage door. He would never remember if it was he who opened the door that day, and it really didn't matter but it is sufficient to know that the door was opened and mother and son watched as the bird tentatively moved to the open portal and then take flight in a swirling whirl of feathers and abandoned bird seed.

His mother returned to the kitchen and after a short while of watching the dervish like mania exhibited by the bird, when it finally alighted in the high corner on the crown of the wall and became inactive or, as a young child would say, boring, he left the room too and returned to the kitchen and his mini fleet of mini vehicles.

Some time elapsed, who knows how much, maybe an hour or two and the time had come to return the bird to its place of both security and captivity. His mother and he began pushing slowly and gradually the lounge door open in case the bird was poised ready and primed to rush from its current location to even more expansive environs.

When there was sufficient space to permit access, they entered, swiftly closing the door behind them. The bird was still static and perched on the crown, shifting its head from side to side as it observed with seeming interest the new arrivals in its midst. One of the significant features of that building in Cressy Road were its high ceilings. Such height furnished the room with a sense of grandeur and expanse for what were essentially not overly spacious sizes. Such height also provided this animal with almost unassailable avoidance ability.

No matter what his mother did, she could not coax, threaten, cajole or succeed in dislodging that bird. All her efforts met with the same outcome. Failure. She climbed on a chair with newspaper in hand attempting to shoo the bird away. Even on the chair, the ceiling was too high for her. She enlisted the services of a broom but as she neared the creature with the threatening implement, it simply flew to another corner of the crown. It was almost as if the rider of the sky was toying with her. As for him, he was helpless to assist, he just watched, periodically issuing words of encouragement or childlike counsel in a bid to create some collaborative alliance.

Before too long, what was initially genuine levity morphed into mild vexation, then increased irritation until finally, blatant distress. Perhaps she was conscious of the time, the hour her husband would be returning, dinner needing to be prepared, Michelle requiring collection or perhaps the dark and burgeoning growth inside her skull was already imperceptibly poisoning her mind with its nefarious intent and purpose and already she was succumbing to its deadly fabric.

Whatever the cause of her increased agitation, he naturally assumed the bird was the source of the problem. He was not used to seeing his mother upset thus, he could not recall years later, ever having even witnessed her shout at him. He loved his mother, he loved her above all things and it was perhaps then, at that moment, when he was driven by an urgent impulsion to ameliorate her discomfort, that the idea rushed in upon him like some ebbing tide given leave to re-visit shore.

'Don't worry, Mummy! I know how to get Cookie down and back in her cage. Wait here a minnit,' he said. And with that he quickly slipped out of the room, carefully negotiating the exit to ensure matters weren't exacerbated, and he disappeared. His mother continued to hurl innocuous venom at the winged thing and probing now and then the crown of the wall with the thick and bushy end of the broom but the bird continued to evade its would be gaoler. The door re-opened and in expectant triumph Danny returned but not alone this time. His mother looked at him and what he was carrying, then looked at the bird and then back towards her only son.

'I'll use the grenade launcher!' he cried with boyish delight and promptly raised his newly acquired Johnny7 to his shoulder ready for the first salvo. The first grenade, it was in fact a ping pong ball but not to unbridled imaginations, missed the mark but evoked a startled movement and a screech of alarm as Cookie deserted its up to then incontestable position of superiority.

His mother went quiet and assumed the role of observer, grateful for assistance or perhaps tired after her own failed efforts. Following four or five volleys, missile shots as well as grenades, the bird must have realised that it had met its match. Nemesis could fly faster than its own small wings could propel it and it must have known there was no haven available that would grant it sanctuary. It finally flew back onto the extended gate of its cage and hopped back into its home.

He felt like a man; he had rescued his mother, he was a warrior and it didn't go unnoticed. As she closed the birdcage, she came over and took him in her arms and squeezed him to her body.

'You clever boy, Dandan,' she said, 'you clever, clever boy. I love you so much!' and with that she kissed his forehead that was draped by the blond locks that were a common thread of her, his sister and himself. He still felt safe and secure at that moment and his smile was as wide as the epitome of width. He was his mother's saviour. But not he, not anyone, not anything, would be able to save her for very much longer.....

~~~~~~~~~~~~~~~~~~~~~~

GERRARD ROAD (part one)

The train pulled into the Angel and the three of them alighted. In 1968 the Angel was one of those tube stations that looking back was really quite dangerous. There was one central island platform serving on one side the northern track and on the other the southern. Furthermore, the platform was very thin relative to the volume of passengers who used it for their daily commute. The Angel station today is unrecognisable from that period and yet in years to come, he would become nostalgic for the 1968 model. It was a station with which he would become extremely familiar. They clambered up the stairs and negotiated the bend at the top and once more used the lift for ascension to street level. There are no lifts there now, they have been replaced by escalators which are the third highest in Western Europe. The Angel station was his gateway to Belsize Park, pub work and the school which would ultimately provide his means of escape from the awfulness of Gerrard Road.

Once at street level, they continued on towards their journey's end, still clutching Martha's hands as though losing hold thereof would see them cast into some abyss of abandon. Quietly they walked. No-one was speaking. Thoughts kept words at bay. They finally arrived. Martha opened the front door with her key and they all entered.

'Come on you two, let's go downstairs,' said Martha. They did, they went downstairs to the basement which housed the kitchen and living room. They entered, two sheepish, lost, confused and unknowing children in the company of unfamiliar family.

This wasn't home. He knew he wanted to be at home. Hampstead flat home. Was Michelle thinking the same? Why was no-one telling them anything? There was Aunty Grace and her mother, his father's mother, also called Grace in that kitchen.

The residual day passed; most of the individual events and words spoken on that day and in that period have long since dissolved into the abyss of nothingness, floated on air and off into virtual aether like dispersing bubbles from a child's toy. At some point presumably his father had arrived and presumably they ate and drank. Would they have remembered that he no longer took sugar in his tea? There could not have been much for those children to do. None of their things were there. Everything was at Cressy Road. His mother was at Cressy Road. He would have wondered at some point whether she ever received that cup of tea but that would have probably seemed an irrelevance of total inconsequence to those adults with more pressing issues on their minds.

The only events that he would remember about that day following their arrival at Gerrard Road were those surrounding bedtime. The adults must have been in concentrated and protracted exchanges in relation to the logistics presented by the advent of three new people into the established structure of an established household framework.

It could not have been an expected interruption even though one would have imagined that it should have been but the reason he knew it was not expected was because of those initial sleeping arrangements.

At some point it must have become clear to him that they would not be going home that night (at this point however, it certainly wasn't clear to him that they would *never* be going home again) and perhaps this clarity arrived when the younger Grace, she must have been in her mid forties, told him to follow her to where he would be sleeping that night.

They left the kitchen, the spinster aunt leading the motherless son. As they emerged from the kitchen which was the hub of the downstairs dwelling, they turned left and ascended four small steps which led to the toilet that occupied a tiny space on its own and then turning back on themselves, a full set of stairs running parallel to the smaller set, leading up to the ground floor, street level. At the top, there was a short passage that led to the front door through which they had entered earlier and two doors sat off the passage on the right, both of which led to two bedrooms, the first, belonging to Aunty Grace, the other to his grandmother. Their climb did not end there, however, and they turned left again up a third set of stairs and then, left again up a fourth where at the top, directly in front was another door whose room would later become the bedroom of his two cousins, Martha's sons, and on the right, another door. There was yet another set of stairs at the top, and another that led to apex of the house, one floor containing two rooms, Martha and Charlie's kitchen and bedroom. But they journey stopped at the door on their right.

Grace opened it and led him in. The light was on and before him lay extended and unoccupied two single beds, each hugging opposite walls with one smaller camp bed taking up position in between its larger and more permanent counterparts. That was to be his bed that first night in Gerrard Road. What would he have worn to bed?

Had someone brought some clothes from Hampstead, prescient of the events that were to unfold that day? All he would remember of that first night however, was following spinster Grace up the stairs, wondering why they were there at all, missing his mother and his Hampstead home. It didn't even feel like an adventure. It was all so out of character and utterly alien to his usual routine.

The next morning, he didn't awake naturally, it was the opening of the door that woke him. Sunlight filled the room and there at the entrance carefully carrying three cups in his hand was Charlie, and as he took in the unfamiliar landscape of the room, he looked to his left and saw one of the permanent beds occupied with a shape depicting human presence and when he turned to view the other, there too lay a person. His cousins. Both reluctant to respond to the morning arousal from their somnolent status. Charlie was by his side, towering above and his first words to young Daniel were not immediately comprehensible.

'Oh, someone's had a small accident I see,' he said so gently and with no hint of remonstration. Danny followed Charlie's eyes for clarification and to his right, on the floor close to his bed, was a surprisingly neat, small mound of indefinable colour which he slowly realised was vomit. He had been sick whilst sleeping. He raised his eyes to the level of the bed next to him. The occupant of the bed on his right, the oldest of the two cousins, whose earlier resistance to the emerging day was now displaced by an almost perverse curiosity at his father's comments, was staring inquisitively, almost transfixed by the small pile.

'I'm sorry.' That's all he said. Gently. Childishly. He was the stranger here. This was not his place. He was the interloper. He felt embarrassed and shamed and frightened. The other three people in that room at that moment were barely known to him. There were no allies there. He was alone. An overwhelming desire to cry engulfed him. He fought it however, as he had no desire to make an even bigger fool of himself in front of these unknown quantities. He had never felt so alone as he did at that moment although he would feel a similar sense of loneliness again. He ran his teeth over his lip in the hope that that would somehow prevent the onset of his tears from welling up and adopting physical form thus betraying his feelings.

Charlie placed the cups on a table by the window at the head of his camp bed and left the room. Seconds later, he re-appeared and bent down to where the contents of the little boy's stomach had been deposited, and with sleeveless arm he produced a cloth and proceeded to clean up the mess.

'It's only a little bit of sick,' he said, still in the same gentle tone, 'all gone now'. Relief replaced shame but the desire to weep didn't recede, just had its origin change.

That first proper introduction to Charlie would prove to be indicative of the man. Those sleeveless arms revealed anchor tattoos, like Popeye, but a genuine sailor who had seen action in the Second World War. He seemed so large that morning but only in the eyes of a child, in reality, he was of small stature but of enormous heart. He was the redeeming feature of Gerrard Road, he was a good thing in a place of few good things. A gentle man, a kind one too.

Danny would spend as much time as he could in those early years in childlike chat with the sailor who laughed when the little boy asked if depth charges were bigger than a football. Charlie who always seemed to be working on the same sludge in the crankcase problem with his car. Charlie who took him and his own sons to kick a football on Hackney Marshes every so often. Charlie who had the misfortune to live in Gerrard Road after the Hampstead three arrived…

~~~~~~~~~~~~~~~~~~~~~

JUMPING THE COINS

It is impossible to know how long had passed from the morning of Danny's first night at Gerrard until the day of the jumping coins. Perhaps a week, perhaps a day or two, he really would never have any idea and once more, as so many other facets of this tale, it really doesn't matter. They were in the kitchen, Michelle and her brother. There was no-one else in the room. That in itself seemed slightly odd. However, Michelle must have viewed the lack of adult presence for opportunity and with that daring bravado that in his seven year old eyes was probably falsely constructed but certainly magnified by the twenty-two month age gap, she quickly devised an excellent pastime.

In the kitchen, against the wall, a four legged drawerless table found itself. It was an old thing by appearance, nondescript, with nothing that stood out other than its ugly demeanour. It looked and felt cheap and its surface, composed of copious and sequential miniscule blue and white dots, in no way diminished its overall appearance of awfulness. However, it was functional as a working top for culinary preparation, and today, the day of the jumping coins, the day his world would collapse about him, today it provided an additional function thanks to the adroit and creative thinking of his sister.

'Dandan,' she began, 'go and get that jar over there, behind you. The one with the copper coins in it.'

'Why?' he said.

'We can play jump the coins,' she replied enthusiastically.

'What's jump the coins?' he enquired.

'Just get them,' she went on, brooking no resistance. He was still in the compliant stage of life, little reason to mistrust nor suspect, so he did as he was bade. 'Give them here,' she instructed. Once more he indulged her command. 'Right,' she said and as she scattered the various coinage, mostly of little value, over the table, carefully separating any that fell contiguous to another. She continued. 'We are goin' to make the coins jump and the one that makes them jump the highest wins.'

'How will we know who makes them jump the highest?' he replied after some small consideration.

'Oh shut up!'she said. 'It'll be obvious.' After a little more measured consideration, he introduced a new obstacle.

'But I don't know how to make them jump!'

'Ok,' came the reassuring reply from a little girl who was intent on putting her plan into action before there could be intervention from external elements, *adult* elements, that would almost certainly bring an end to the design she had in mind. 'I'll show you what to do.' Not that it was a game she had ever played before. Her improvisation was outstanding.

He stepped back to allow her space.

'Ready?' she asked.

'Yes,' he replied.

'Ok, watch me.' He watched. He watched as Michelle primed herself, pursed her lips and then, shoulders slightly inclined, with a fury beyond her years, began pounding the table with her fists. The coins began to rise. The noise was deafening. The table was actually rising slightly from the floor. He expected adult entry any second. There was none. How could they not be hearing this? It was astonishing. Still the pounding continued. He was hypnotised by the motion. First his eyes hovered on the coins, then to his sister's nine year old hands and then her taut and focused face and then back to the coins. They really were jumping! And she was *really* good. They were leaping high up, far from the blue white platform of launch. She really was good. He was totally captivated by the activity.

A voice said something, her voice but it was inaudible above the banging of her fists, the clattering of the coins and the repeated thudding of the table legs every time they landed on the kitchen floor.

'WHAT DID YOU SAY?' he shouted.

'JOIN IN!' came the reply. Join in. Yes. The desire to join in was irresistible. He knew this must have been naughty but it looked like so much fun! There was no longer any relevance to, nor interest in competition.

It didn't matter about who could launch the coins the highest, it was no longer about winning, it was about pure, undiluted fun in a game that had no purpose nor aim, simply about making noise, BANG BANG BANG, and making the coins jump.

He joined in. Michelle and Danny stood side by side, their hands almost in unison rising up and down on that ugly table, beating it with painful force, making those coins jump higher and higher, totally immersed in that mindless and yet joy giving activity. Briefly, for an unknown quantity of time, his mind was immune to any unsavoury thoughts, immune to any considerations about recent events that had conspired to result in his presence by that table that day. Briefly, he was happy again. For a moment, his world was whole once more and life was without issue. He should have savoured this. Had he known what was about to unfold, he *would* have savoured it. He would have clung to it. For dear life. This could have been the last moments of his young life when he was truly happy, even for those seconds of inane and banal fun, before the devastation of what had happened would be brought into the light of his awareness.

The door opened and Martha appeared; if she was cross with the clattering of the coins and banging of fists, she disguised it very well. The two siblings desisted immediately and stared in dumb silence at her, waiting for some reaction to the cacophony that they had created, with the only noise breaking the silence being those coins which had climbed loftier than the rest and then falling tardily back to earth with a shrill clanking under the irresistible force of gravity.

'Danny,' she said, 'your father wants you, he is in the living room.'

'Ok,' he said and made his way to the room which was adjacent to the kitchen on the right.

He entered the room which was always quite dark even on the brightest of summer days, an obscurity due to its basement location. The only window was overlooked by the street outside where the mobile legs of passing pedestrians seemed amputated from the rest of their bodies to the observers below. His father was sitting on an armchair on the right of the door and close to it. The little boy realised that the seated man must have been there the entire time that he and his sister had been launching coins into space. Presumably he was no longer able to tolerate the din and was about to express his anger. Why just him though, why not Michelle too? Martha must have left since the noise from the kitchen had started up again which meant his sister was continuing to exploit the window of opportunity that had presented itself. However, the noise that carried seemed more muffled now that it was just the one person at the head of mission control.

He looked at his father who was looking towards the window that punctured the wall in front of him. His father said nothing and seemed quite distant. By his side, on the floor was a tumbler which contained the brownish liquid that he had often seen in Hampstead, the liquid that began with *H*. His eyes searched for dimpled glass but there was no bottle in sight.

'Daddy?' he enquired.

His father looked up at him. 'Come closer, Danny,' he said in a low voice, soft and gentle, not at all like a command and as he did so he extended his hands and took hold of those of his son which were slightly reddened from their recent exertions; he pulled him close to him. The man was still seated, the boy standing right in front of him, both connected as one by the clasping of hands.

'I have something to tell you,' he continued.

What could it be, thought the boy? The tone of his father's words had removed any concern that it could be anger at the bouncing game. His father's eyes were totally concentrated on his own and he noticed the hint of tears that glistened within and moistened them without.

'Your mummy has had to go away,' he began and without pause continued, 'up to heaven with the angels.'

Years later he supposed this was probably as effective and as palliative a delivery of such devastating news as any other. How does a surviving parent tell a young child that their mother or father has died? Years later he also realised it must have been one of the most heartbreaking tasks for his father, breaking that news. Initially nothing seemed to happen.

Then slowly, without ability to control, without concern for consequence or observer, the flood of tears that he felt building somewhere down deep, deep inside burst through the ineffectual dam of his eyes and drowned his cheeks as he began to sob immeasurably. He felt the grasp of his father's hands tighten. He wasn't looking at his father. He was looking above his head at the wall beyond. He couldn't take it all in, he couldn't process the ramifications.

What did this mean? That he would never see his beloved mother again? How could that be? If *only* he hadn't dropped those books.

He looked down at his father again, his face contorted with the agony of the weeping, the unstoppable weeping, and despite his own devastation, he saw that his father's eyes were themselves now awash with tears.

His father pulled him down to his level and cuddled him with as much force as he could, careful not to hurt him. After a few seconds or maybe more, he released him.

'Danny, you can go back to Michelle now,' giving him a kiss on the cheek as he finished. The boy who had just been given the most devastating news that he could have ever have been given, still crying, wordlessly left his father in that lugubrious, dark room, with only whisky to keep him company, and went back into the kitchen. Michelle was still furiously jumping the coins but threw a glance in his direction as he appeared.

'Why are you crying?' she asked almost disinterestedly.

'Daddy just told me Mummy has died,' he answered, still sobbing heavily.

'Oh that,' she said. 'He told me ages ago and I barely cried at all.' He would later believe that despite her tender years, that was her way of alleviating his visible distress.

No matter what he was thinking, no matter what he would think, at that moment, he pulled up his trousers, rubbed his tear filled eyes brusquely with his sleeve and alongside his sister, began to jump coins again. However, the boy that played now would never again be the same boy as the one that had played before.

~~~~~~~~~~~~~~~~~~~~~

GRACE THE ELDER

Nan. That was Grace the Elder. The cohesive force of his father's family. Mother of seven, one of whom had died in infancy, grandmother to many more. Her husband, Arthur, the unspeakable, the never to be mentioned pariah in the family who had taken his own life many years before, long before he could become acquainted with his grandchildren. His miserable and desperate end was a fact jealously guarded, not publicly disseminated nor advertised, not discussed, not known to most of the grandchildren. It was almost as if the man *himself* were the secret.

Who knows if it was the ignominious ending of his life or the hardship and difficulty that doubtless beset his surviving spouse with so many mouths to feed that elevated him to such levels of tacit anathema. The enduring reality was that she had reared and cultivated a throng of children alone, in an era where state benefits offered no safety net, an age when children oft times left school at 14 and substituted revenue production for any potential further education. The two eldest of her clan of offspring, Bernard and Grace, would have certainly been shouldered with a relatively heavy burden very early on in their lives in the pursuit of the financial wherewithal required for basic survival.

What irony then, what terribly tragic and unpredictable irony, that years later his nan would once more have similar responsibility foisted upon her by death, and the subsequent arrival of the surviving incumbents of Cressy Road, albeit some twenty years after the first event.

Danny really didn't know her well, his tender years or scant regular contact or maybe a combination of them both explaining the lack of intimacy or the lack of its memory. He could recall with clarity though, her look, her bespectacled visage, her elderly manner. That mac that served as her protective outer layering, lingered in vibrant memory as did the trademark beret, her chosen form of headgear as opposed to Grace's and Martha's penchant for the in vogue scarves about their pate. He could recall how she and Martha would make the daily ritual pilgrimage to Chapel Market to purchase victuals for their respective households, separate under the same roof, demarcated by an invisible parallel which was located on the first stair of the final two flights of the house.

He could only assume that she, in her role as his sister's and his own grandmother would not have resented the presence of those semi-orphans in her midst, notwithstanding the imposition and the interruption of the established equilibrium that such a presence represented. Indeed, as stern as she could be, or as stern as he would have understood stern from his youthful and timid perspective, he could not recall any episodes (bar one) or examples of aggressive behaviour that overall would suggest anything other than a welcoming if resigned stance on her part.

Other than the imagery of his grandmother, there were only a handful of actual events involving her that he would be able to recall. The precise chronological order was vague but what was indubitable was that they all took place in the first two years of his arrival. One of the memories found him in the living room, the room next to the kitchen, in that basement where they spent their non sleeping time whilst residents of Gerrard. Use of bedrooms as places other than for nocturnal repose was not permitted. On that occasion, the kitchen, as he recalled, was occupied by his grandmother, Michelle and BT and maybe one of the aunts. He had no idea what he was doing in the living room but the door opened and there appeared his grandmother, shoving Michelle into the room away from the kitchen dwellers. Taking his sister by the shoulders, she immediately set to the frenetic and energetic task of repeatedly shaking the young girl roughly back and forth. He was shocked by the severity of the motion but his sister remained insolently impervious throughout.

Another incident later afforded him some insight as to what had been the cause of the earlier rigorous exhibition of undisguised anger. He, Michelle and BT were in the lounge, all facing the TV, when his grandmother opened the door behind them and beckoned quietly to Michelle who along with her brother had looked to see who had entered. BT remained focused on the screen and wasn't interested in the entrant and was out of the eye line of the older woman. It was likely that Michelle had committed some transgression, almost certainly minor, and her grandmother wanted to remonstrate with her in private, perhaps in a similar fashion to the one described previously. However, as would became clear in *that* house, any 'dirty washing' was never laundered in front of BT or indeed, in front of anyone outside that house.

So, the audacious derring-do of his sister was heroically amplified in his eyes when to his amused amazement but serious concern, she turned her gaze away from the old woman who was still beckoning her with increasing intensity, mouthing a silent 'Michelle' here and there in such a way that would have alerted no-one not conversant with the process to the escalating wrath and utter frustration mounting inside her. Michelle was perfectly aware of what Michelle was doing; she was either indescribably bold since this blatant disregard for her grandmother's instruction could only create ever worsening consequences or she was thinking only in the moment, oblivious to the terrible risk she was running. Whichever it was, she knew full well, that whilst BT was in that room, unaware of the drama being played out behind him, nothing unsavoury nor untoward would happen. She seemed totally blinkered to the absolute certainty that the unknowing shield of her well being would not be in the room all day and she would eventually be without his unconscious protection…

This event then, caused him to believe that something similar had occurred in the earlier incident when once more Michelle had found herself in the proximity of that unwitting field of protection except on that occasion , somehow his grandmother had succeeded in dislodging her from the mantle of security and then once out of earshot and view, offloaded her excessive assault with impunity.

The next memory involved him. This occurred in the period following his re-location from the bedroom that he had been sharing with his two cousins to the bedroom which he shared with his father. It was the room closest to the front door. He loved that period of sharing with his father.

He would recall fondly the rare but treasured occasions when a late night feast would take place, a midnight feast long after he should have been anesthetised by soporific onslaughts. He would wait patiently, resisting as hard as he was able the full attack of that slumber, relentless in its persistency, with his ears straining to detect the earliest indication of his father's arrival and on those occasions when he managed to resist sleep's seductive calling, they together, father and son, would dine mischievously late on a banquet of Fry's chocolate and Marathon bars, or maybe chewy sweets and Maltesers, under the blankets which was illuminated by a cheap torch, the product of his father's prescient preparation.

It was a summer evening and was still light, light enough to permit reading without the aid of a lamp, a fortuitous coincidence considering that throughout his young life at Gerrard Road he would never be allowed a lamp in his bedroom for reasons quite unfathomable to him, then and later. He was aware that he was breaking the rules that estival evening since bedtime had to be observed with an unswervable adherence, and reading, once ensconced in bed, was absolutely prohibited.

That evening Danny was breaking the rules; given his compliant character partly shaped by innate gentility that he would always believe was inherited from his father's own gentil and inherently placid manner, and partly shaped by the events of the recent past which now triggered some subconscious instinct deep inside that told him to maintain a low a profile as possible and to cause no friction nor disturbance, it was unlike him to infringe a rule.

However, an ever increasing love of reading books, the origins of which he would never be able to identify, must have been a greater force than the preoccupation of this infraction, an infraction which frankly seemed quite innocuous.

It was likely that he was reading about a tomboy called George with a canine called Timmy with five or maybe seven covert children encountering adventure after adventure. Absorbed as he was by whatever subject matter was gluing him to the pages, he was conscious of the light that was beginning to fade and whose ultimate expiration would signal the conclusion of his reading for that day. He was also keeping one ear primed to hear any noise that might issue from the kitchen or living room down below where the two Graces would be that would alert him to any approach to his bedroom door and discovery of his venial behaviour.

His shock and horror can only be imagined then, when with a turn of foot that belied her age, in the doorway was standing his grandmother; with a rapidity that unfortunately failed to replicate that of the older woman, he was on his side in a flash and book deposited under the bed with what he hoped was adequate alacritous deftness whilst simultaneously assuming the position and manner of a dozing child. His mind raced. How had he not heard her he thought, how had he not discerned a creaking stair that would serve to betray her imminent arrival? She must have seen him reading. There could be no doubt she had witnessed his transgression.

That gradual extinguishing of the light whose arrival only moments before he had prayed would be delayed for as long as possible was now replaced with an equally fervent prayer in which he pleaded for total darkness to fall with immediate effect so that somehow he would be swallowed up in the murky depths of night and consequently become invisible.

He kept his eyes closed for what seemed like an eternity but was almost certainly no more than thirty seconds. He was holding his breath, he was playing possum, and not one sound could be heard in that room. Perhaps she had gone, he thought. She surely would have said something by now had she still been present. Finally, with a supreme effort of will, terrified that any movement in him or the landscape would elicit unthinkable consequences, he turned onto his back and opened his eyes in the direction of the door. He stiffened. She was still there. Staring right at him. Expressionless. Then, with not a word emerging from her lips, she walked towards him, bent over, picked up the book from under the bed and walked out of the room. He rolled over and unsure whether that was the end of it, he eventually fell into a troubled sleep.

~~~~~~~~~~~~~~~~~~~~~~

THREE SCHOOLS

In the two years or so that followed those final halcyon days at Cressy Road, things to a certain degree began to settle down into some sort of recognisable pattern. The initial upheaval was a terrible schism, especially for young hearts, and established stability replaced by a future bereft of a solid maternal platform was not without difficulty, not least logistically. His father continued to work for the London Underground in the same shift patterns as before with a fairly seamless progression. As for Michelle and Danny, initially Martha would take them to school every day, back and forth to Belsize Park re-tracing the same steps that had led them in the first place to Gerrard Road one fateful October evening. Needless to say, this arrangement could not endure indefinitely; it was a long trip for two young children, exacerbated by its frequency and it was extremely time consuming for their aunt. So behind the scenes, the adults were obviously considering alternative options which would produce a regimen of a less demanding kind.

Inevitably it came to pass and one morning, when school time beckoned, instead of heading towards the now familiar halls of the Angel station, their direction took a very different turn.

'Where are we going, Aunty Martha?' asked Danny. Another day, another question, the same protagonists.

'Today I am taking you to your new school,' she said trying to inject an element of contagious excitement into her words. They both looked up at her as one. New school?

'But we already have a school!' Michelle said and Danny nodded furiously in agreement, repeating her comment.

'Yes, we already have a school!'

'What about our own school?' continued his sister.

'You will like this school more, it is nearer, we can walk, so we won't have to use those smelly old trains again.'

'But what about all our friends?' enquired Danny, in an increasingly panicked tone.

'You will make new friends,' came the pragmatic reply.

'But we like our friends, we know our friends well, they come to our parties,' he said, unaware that the use of the collective *we* was a subliminal mechanism to elicit group support and equally unaware when he said *come* and not *came* that there would be no more parties like those that had graced the Johnny7 episode.

'We are going to your new school and that's final,' stated Martha, seeking to put an end to anymore puerile rebellion.

'But we don't want to go to a new school,' insisted Danny and this time it was his sister's head shaking in assent. In his mind though, he knew he was powerless, both he and his sister, they had absolutely no influence, no power to resist adult dictates.

'Will I never see DingDong again?' he spluttered, tears once more rising from somewhere deep down inside, panicking at the thought that his best friend was in immediate danger of being consigned to the bowels of indifferent irrelevance. Surely he wasn't going to lose him, his best friend as well as his mother. He was visibly crying now, but not loudly. There was no point making a scene, this he had come to understand and he didn't want people seeing him upset. He was impotent in the face of adult will and intent. These weren't conscious thoughts so much as behaviour he was coming to learn.

'Yes, you will see DingDong again,' said Martha. But he never would.

The moment he arrived at St Peter's and Paul's, he was never going to like it. He was used to the Rosary, his teachers, his friends and their playground frolics and frivolous games that they all took so seriously. And nor did the foreboding gate that welcomed them lubricate the wheels of gradual assimilation and fondness for what would one day be an alma mater. Not *the* alma mater, but *a,* one of three. He would never remember much of the time spent within the walls of this educational institution but that could also be a consequence of the very limited time that this would be his place of learning. He could remember the rectangular playground though, split on two levels separated by a bank running its entire length comprising three elongated steps. Those of a certain age, presumably five to eight year olds were entitled only to play on the upper level whilst the rest, the eights to eleven year olds, had as their domain the lower region.

He didn't know anyone there and no-one knew him; the various trysts would now long be established, alliances well and truly forged and best friendships by this point cemented in childlike rigidity. He was an interloper, an outsider, with no history nor common sense of purpose nor play. He remembered standing against a tree during playtimes at the far reaches of the square, neither playing nor engaging nor interacting; he just stood there, hands in pockets, blond thick hair wild, signalling the beginning of its curly future, propped up by the tree as he kicked the toe of his shoe against the hard surface beneath as though he were striving nonchalantly to burrow below its surface. Many times his grandmother would castigate him for continually scuffing his shoes but it didn't prevent him from persisting. He hated that school. Hated it.

Years later his sister would tell him that when she was in the midst of some game or another, hopscotch more likely than not, she would catch sight of him and disengaging from the activity, come to the bottom of the steps. Unable to cross that divide, she strove to gain his attention waving her arms and calling to him but so intent was he on his burrowing enterprise, that he was not aware of her overtures.

She would then stand there herself, close to tears seeing her brother all by himself even though a throng of carefree, happy children were at play all around him, and she wished that she could ascend those stairs herself and happily offer her services as his willing playmate. The next time Martha led them to yet another different school, Danny did not protest once. Not a word.

St John the Evangelist would be his and his sister's final primary school. It was so much more welcoming than the previous. An open front, no prison like gate buttressed by a walled perimeter. There was no divide, no Berlin Wall barrier separating one child from another. His relief of having been liberated from the previous school was so enormous that it relegated his longing for the Rosary to lesser leagues. St John might never replace his first and best school but it would surely be infinitely preferable to the misery that had pervaded him throughout his brief sojourn in the previous establishment.

His attitude from the outset lent itself to a much more gratifying outcome. It could have been the case however, that what shrouded the previous school in such a mantle of abhorrence and unhappiness was that it represented both the surgeon's knife and the resulting bandaging as the residual links to Cressy Road and his mother and the whole of his earthly experience to date were cut away and removed with such ruthless finality. That wound had to some extent healed by the time St Johns opened its doors to these newcomers. His academic landscape at least would now be constructed on a fundament of stability and would serve as a sturdy platform for his cerebral development. Furthermore, clearer memories would be formulated and attach more readily to his conscious lining, more likely due to his increasing age than any delight at his new circumstances.

Such a memory involved Sandro who would become his corporal in the playground skirmishes when little boys, girls too, would simulate the roles played out in battle and war, bloodied knees and exhausted legs and the *bang bang I got you first* emphatic demands which often met with stubborn refusal to take their shots and die, but ultimately a victimless game ready to be played out again and again day after day.

There were normally two groups that formed up ready for the melee, both led by a *Martin* (no connection to his cousin), one of big build with bushy ginger hair whose freckled face always seemed to wear a wide grin but whose sheer physical size qualified him perfectly for leadership duties. He wasn't a bully, it was simply that his corporeal presence brooked no opposition, no resistance to his will. His group comprised the same type as him although not at as commanding anatomically, a similar would be domineering attitude permeating their collective character, more brutish and direct with little or no subtlety or élan.

The other Martin was the antithesis of the first; smaller, but lean and fast, straight dark hair and a quietly confident personality, making up for what he lacked in size and strength with a smooth but natural panache and likeable charm whilst retaining a distance that prevented the favouring of any one individual. Such a manner promoted him effortlessly above all equals. Every boy wanted to be his best friend for which reason he commanded undying loyalty without trying nor knowing it, and his group, like the first, consisted of like minded fellows but not to the same levels of appeal as its leader. To this group Danny attached himself but not at its heart but as a lone soldier on the flanks away from the core.

It was one such day when Sandro, seemingly another loner but in need of at least *one* close ally, approached him.

'Can I be on your side?' Danny gave him a quick once over and unused to such spontaneous requests, simply said,

'OK. But I'm Sarge and you can be my corporal.'

'Ok, Sarge!' the boy replied, smiling enthusiastically. As the game unfolded and they ran round on the flanks picking off unsuspecting enemy stragglers, it came to Danny's attention that Sandro's gun was not the normal type of gun.

'Corp, why is your gun like that?' he enquired, genuinely inquisitive.

'I don't know how to make it like yours and the others',' he said very flatly.

Danny couldn't help but laugh out loud, not sarcastically nor with nasty intent; it just seemed such a ridiculous thing to say. After all, *every* schoolboy and probably schoolgirl too, knew how to turn the palm of their preferred hand down, flat facing the ground, then invert it forty five degrees right if a right hander, left if a leftie and simply fold away the fourth and little finger and what remained was a two fingered gun with thumb acting as the hammer and cocking mechanism, *click click*. What could he possibly mean he didn't know how to do it?

'But Corp, you have turned your hand the right way but you have kept all your fingers out, so it's like a four fingered gun!'

He took hold of his subordinate's sweaty, grimy hand with its extended fingers and with his own, he curled back the two fingers that had to be put away. When Sandro witnessed what was left, pure delight bathed his entire face in visible joy.

'OHHHHH, *that's* how you do it!! Thanks, Sarge, thanks a lot!' he cried and with that, enthusiastically saluted his enlightener, totally unconscious of the presence of the shadowy figure who had crept up behind him.

'BANG, BANG, YOU'RE DEAD. Take your shots!!!' a voice roared into his ear.

Danny was to pass the next three years of his scholarly progression in that place; he would make friends there, albeit conditional on the previous dictates that established relations were entrenched and he would be a latecomer and an outsider but it was a role that he would come to value and cultivate more and more throughout his life's journey. On the periphery of the social fabric, as young child and older man, dipping into the mainstream only when he wanted or needed. For this reason he would never have a best friend there, he had learnt that nothing was fixed and even the most secure relationships were tenuous and arbitrary. He didn't intend to make the same mistake again, although he didn't yet know it but actually once more he would let someone in some three decades later. Still, he would eventually find it quite pleasant there, on that periphery, that circular fringe, safe and self-sufficient, but his emotional detachment and alienation wasn't yet quite complete. The imminent loss of another mother however, would set the scene for the final steps in that process....

~~~~~~~~~~~~~~~~~~~~~~~~

A CALF RUBBING

In the two years following the death of his mother, his life and that of his father, sister and those residents of the lower regions of Gerrard Road underwent profound changes. The schooling was an obvious illustration of this as were the various bedroom modifications. For a while it seemed to him that people in the lower half of that house were forever swapping bedrooms, like some grown up game of musical chairs. The fact was however, that the bedroom for him was just that, a room with a bed in it where he slept. He was never allowed to play in it regardless of which room it happened to be that day, he wasn't even allowed to *be* in it if it weren't bed time, and he was compelled to share whatever baggage and stuff was already in situ within.

He had no lamp so he could not even indulge his escalating love of reading as a pre-bed indulgence unless it was summer which explained why in the summer months, he would go to bed early to exploit the light, even when his age qualified him for much later hours. He didn't have his own cupboard or wardrobe, nor desk or shelves, he simply had a drawer for the foldable items of clothing and one side of a wardrobe for those that required a hanger. That was the sum total of his bedroom. It wasn't that the rooms were sparsely furnished, in fact, the complete opposite was the case. Every room, not just bedrooms, had copious amounts of furniture housed within it, bordering on clutter, more items to gather dust. It was just that he was essentially a guest; and he would remain a guest for the best part of fifteen years until the day Grace asked for his key back. As though he ever needed reminding, that did remind him that it was never really his home.

The arrival of the three from Hampstead had unexpected consequences for one of the other occupants of the downstairs element of the house. BT. Bernard Thomas, the brother of his paternal grandmother who was living there with the spinster and her mother. In return for paying them a stipend, the two women would cook and give him lodging. Predominantly, it was his sister, Grace the Elder who did most of that culinary preparation since Grace the Younger had and retained throughout, a full time job in the optical business, specifically the fabrication of spectacle frames.

Danny didn't know BT at all well; he was just some elderly, bald gentleman who dressed in a rather dapper manner and seemed a very polished and well to do chap. Every Sunday night, at the same hour, he would rise from his armchair in the living room, deposit his glasses on the shelf and then disappear to his room for some considerable time. He would return eventually, dressed to the nines, studiously replace his glasses, then depart the building and disappear for the evening. Danny always wondered what mystical and magical location beckoned this well dressed epicurean and sometimes he would enjoy imagining all the distant possibilities. Years later when he looked back, he realised that the cause of BT's absence, the earthly Nirvana that drew him with dogmatic regularity, was almost certainly a pub.

The Sunday night ritual would not continue for long however, since after some long and protracted discussions one evening inside the nerve centre -the kitchen- of the downstairs household, there was a coup of sorts and BT was invited to leave on the basis that there was not sufficient space now that more indigent family members had arrived.

It was obviously not the direct fault of Michelle or Danny that BT was in all but name evicted from his home but nonetheless, it was indirectly causal. It is true that it could be seen that he had been sacrificed because of the need for space, to make place for them but there was always a current of belief, an underlying sentiment, a rumour that never went away, that the elders wanted to remove BT from the environment in any event and this new set of circumstances provided the ideal excuse. It seemed cruel and heartless nonetheless and Danny wondered were BT went but never established the whereabouts of his next dwelling. He did see BT again, now and then he would appear at the intermittent family events at which Danny himself would intermittently appear later in life. But he and BT shared a communal cause for their more frequent absence than presence at such affairs, namely, Gerrard Road. BT was embittered and resentful was the tacit understanding, about that abrupt eviction and removal from what had been his home for many years and would never forgive the perpetrators of the deed. The explanation for Danny's infrequent attendances were the panic attacks that would slowly descend upon him as a consequence of the childhood yet to unfold fully. One result of BT's removal was Danny's transfer into his father's bed for the time being. Another was the removal of one of the remaining shields of the protective force field that served as some protection for Michelle and Danny. It wouldn't be too much longer before the principal and remaining shield dissolved too.

There were also more subtle ramifications of the death of Danny's mother that peppered this transitional period which were not immediately apparent.

One example of such was the day that their teacher distributed large strips of paper and thick tipped felt pens and told her class of eight and nine year olds that it would be a lovely idea to prepare a personalised, hand made card for the upcoming Mothering Day Sunday. Clearly a delicate situation. A choice between cancelling the idea in its entirety for the sake of one bereft child or subordinating the good of the one for the interests of the many.

'Ok, children,' said the instructor of fertile minds, 'as Danny hasn't got a mummy anymore, he is going to make a nice card for his daddy instead.' 'Lucky daddy!' she went on. 'He will get TWO cards this year! What a lucky daddy to have such a thoughtful son!'

Such a brilliant handling of the situation, to make Danny seem special in *not* having a mummy, to be different from the others, to be the envy of the rest of the class! They were probably all wishing at that moment that they didn't have a mummy either. The truth of the matter was it made no impact on him at all, he didn't even allocate time nor thought to the fact that he had no mother to whom he could deliver this irrelevance. At least that's how he would recall the truth of the matter. And he really was sure it was the truth; he just didn't care about it. What *possible* relevance could a card have He did wonder though, if Michelle's class was at the moment as equally envious of her as his was of him.

If the radical changes that had been forged by the death of Danny's mother were the first and most substantial emotional earthquake, then the death of his grandmother certainly paved the way for the second more insidious tremor.

As different as his life was now, he was gradually adjusting and despite his loss still keen and fresh, Gerrard Road wasn't yet the experience of unendurable horror that it would become. The relative stability can be attributed to the matriarchal presence and potency of his grandmother, Grace the Elder who with all her severity and authoritarian manner, a woman who herself had an exterior hardened on the knocks of her own life, was underlying a loving mother and kindly woman. One morning before school in the immediate aftermath of Cressy Road, he was sitting at the table with his breakfast before him and behind him, in the ever present, plastic armchair that was an enduring feature of the kitchen, sat his nan as most days she sat. They were alone in the room. He was aware of her presence there behind him but was facing away from her with the cerealised fodder before him.

Something came over him; he couldn't eat, he didn't want to go to school. He just suddenly felt so terribly sad and empty and began to cry. He wasn't aware of making any noise but in the quietness of the moment, it wouldn't have been difficult to determine that he was distressed.

'Eat your breakfast,' said his nan.

'I'm not hungry,' he mumbled in between his muffled sobs.

'What's wrong with you?' she asked gruffly. With that, never once leaving his chair, he spun round, wrapped his arms about the shoulders of his seated grandmother and just sobbed and sobbed uncontrollably into her body. She held him in return, saying nothing, but gently patting him on the back in a *there, there* type sentiment. He didn't go to school that day.

The last day he would ever be in the same room with her, the day he stood over by the kitchen door, the day she was once more sitting in that chair, that was a very different kind of day. He had been to school and was still in his school uniform. There were other people in the room but he wouldn't be able to remember who was present. Martha, maybe Grace, his father, Michelle? A matter of insignificance.

He was standing by the door and was observing his grandmother, her eyes open and aware but dulled by the dying of the light of life that wasn't too far from extinction. She was still sufficiently in control of her faculties but they had begun to ebb away. This was the second time in two years that he was in the very close proximity of a dying woman. This time however, very different emotions and feelings were evoked from him. He didn't really care that much; there was simply no comparison. He may not even have realised how compromised was her health. It wasn't that he was wilful in his indifference, it was more a case of less to grieve. There was no long standing relationship, no conspicuous memories, no feeling of genuine love and affection.

He was almost certainly not entertaining these thoughts that day though, they would come later; he was much more likely thinking about childish things, things that didn't involve death, loss, finality and sadness.

Suddenly, his thoughts, whatever they may have been, were abruptly interrupted by a conscious awareness of her focused gaze, as though she were inspecting him, and then he remembered something abruptly and concern took hold of him.

Slowly, with almost indiscernible movements, he began raising his right foot up along the back of his left calf, hoping that once there, it would give the impression of scratching some irritating itch. Despite her waning lucidity, the movement caught her eye and she looked down to its origin. He had successfully manoeuvred his foot out of sight behind the other leg and began rubbing it up and down in a scratching simulation. He wasn't thinking about her dying or being unwell at that moment, he was just hoping that she hadn't caught sight of the scuffed shoe, a habit of great irritation to her. There was nothing he could do about the remaining floor bound foot however, and when she moved her eyes from the one to the other, he waited apprehensively for the reaction. She then raised her eyes to look at his face but just like once before, not a word left her lips. It was then he realised she must be very, very unwell.

~~~~~~~~~~~~~~~~~~~~~~~

FALLOUT

The death of his grandmother heralded significant but gradual changes. One such alteration was his final transfer to the bedroom which would remain the same for the rest of his occupancy. One evening, he was told that he would be sleeping in a different room that night and no longer lodge with his father. As a few years before, once more he found himself being led up the stairs wondering what would be his destination this time. As he continued climbing, he began to think he was heading to the top, where Martha and Charlie and the boys lived, the top floor reflecting the basement in room number and layout, kitchen and lounge which at night doubled up as Martha and Charlie's bedroom.

But he didn't continue to the apex, it was to be the room where he had spent his first ever night in that house but this time, minus his two cousins who were now sharing the adjacent room to his new quarters. His father was now alone in the bedroom on the ground floor nearest the front door and Michelle would be sharing with her aunt Grace in the room next to that. There would only be one more modification to this design and that would be as a direct result of an illness not too far distant in the future.

The most severe, *initial* consequence by far however, was the emotional collapse of his aunt Grace. Of course, as was to be expected, her other sons and daughters, six in total including Grace, were distraught and deeply saddened by their mother's death but Grace was the hardest hit. Without question.

This wasn't that astonishing considering the symbiotic relationship of the two. With the exception of the younger Grace, all of his grandmother's offspring were married with children of their own, although his own father was now a widower. Danny's aunt Grace was a committed spinster, childless and without partner, with a reasonable job and who had been sharing a home, the nether regions of Gerrard Road predominantly, with her mother. Her mother to her was the equivalent of the immediate families of her siblings to them. They spent the evenings together, shared the weekends as one and found more or less total emotional solace in the other's existence. Not surprising at all then, that the death of her mother had such a profound and more destructive effect on her than the others.

In the early days following her mother's demise, when the initial substitutes were now full time replacements and the constitution of the downstairs was now finalised which comprised his father, himself, Michelle and Grace, evenings would be mostly spent in the living room. A dark, dank prison like basement with plastic furnishings that didn't match, antiquated items that were antiquated even then, pictures that adorned the walls that appeared sepia in tone (when Grace one day gently cleaned them, the only time in his fifteen years residence in that place that they ever *were* cleaned, to his absolute amazement, the brown sea of seeming sepia was transformed into a translucent blue), that was their living room. Their father, when he wasn't on shifts, Michelle and Danny would sit watching the television, while Grace would lie supine on one of the settees dozing fitfully, and without warning, at unpredictable intervals, would suddenly call out for her mother.

She would wake herself up with such exclamations, sit up and then return to her former position until the next utterance aroused her once more and the pattern repeated.

Michelle and Danny would turn to observe this unintentional performance with mild amusement, both too young to be empathic or indeed, sympathetic despite their own relatively recent experience of bereavement. Their father seemed oblivious to the spectacle, perhaps he could endure no longer the sight of distressed women extended on couches or chairs or perhaps he had no sympathy or compassion left to give.

How long this went on is hard to remember or quantify but gradually it eased and Grace began to return to a more balanced level of functionality. There was much more for her to do now though; with her mother alive, much of the burden of cooking for three new arrivals in addition to the three already in situ had been shared. Now, as well as maintaining a full time job, Grace alone was responsible for feeding four people breakfast and dinner. She never asked for this; but then, neither did those young children. Years later, when Grace died, having outlived all her brothers and sisters, at her funeral, accolades of heroism were vocalised. Danny wouldn't even bother going and people wondered why. With retrospect, this could be seen as the period when the resentment began to germinate within her breast which ultimately bursted out in vitriolic bloom.

It would have been insidious at first, testing the water; little things that would easily go unnoticed, a petty row leading to an escalating situation when insults would fly, voices raised but then die down and peter out.

There were eight people now within those Angelic walls, the family upstairs, Martha, Charlie and their two sons and of course downstairs there resided himself, his father, sister and Aunty Grace. The rows generally were restricted to the downstairs contingent (with one notable exception), with the conflict rarely spilling over into the wider arena of the whole house. The family upstairs were much more of a contained entity and yet free to 'drop in' downstairs at will. This arrangement was not however, a two-way street. Martha was, understandably, very guarded of her family's right and desire for self containment. After all, they were a *proper* family and other than the absence of a physical door two flights down from the top, to all intents and purposes, theirs was a separate flat.

Whenever one of those above needed to minister to their toiletry requirements, they would have to descend the stairs from the top to the only toilet in the house and often, primal business concluded, they would drop down the last four steps and enter the kitchen. As with all exposure to continual repetition, it became second nature for Danny to recognise which upstairs incumbent was en route to the bowels of the house.

Philip, the youngest, but five years older than Danny, would launch himself from the outset, signalling his approach from practically his first step, thundering down fast, energetic, eliciting groans and creaks from the old, dilapidated floor boards. Martin was more refined, gambolling down with the gait of a delicate gazelle, rhythmic and almost lyrical, neither walking nor sprinting.

Martha had a pedestrian carriage which although not conspicuous in itself, was attributable to her because the others were so distinct that she could be identified simply because she wasn't one of them; and then Charlie. That gentle man had a style of walking to mirror his nature. Often Danny didn't hear him until the very last flight was acquired and even then, not always, and often it was only the betrayal of the toilet chain that would ultimately confirm his categorical presence. Stealth like, slow and deathly quiet.

When the initial rows erupted, the principal antagonist was normally Grace although in the early days, Martha was her cohort and ally. The rest of Martha's clan remained above, if not oblivious to, then at least sheltered from the voluble sounds rising up from below. His father would be the object of Grace's venomous outbursts, probably replicating years of sibling behavioural interaction, from childhood and beyond but regardless of its precedent, it was very current then. Danny and his sister were too young to take active part and much of the content of the early exchanges has long been forgotten but that there was acrimony and ill will from the spinster was unforgettable. He didn't recall alcohol featuring predominantly at this juncture but its increasing presence became more and more pronounced as the years rolled by.

The first prodigious explosion of the harboured bitterness aimed specifically at Danny and his sister happened shortly after the final bedding amendments. By this time Danny was nine and his sister eleven and they were now full blooded alumni of St John's. His father was on shift work, the late turn or the middle turn maybe, but whichever turn, not present. Danny was downstairs in the kitchen or living room and it must have been around the early bedtime that he had come to cultivate which normally arrived at eight o'clock.

Presently, he heard some noise emanating from the floor above and moving towards the door, he pulled it ajar to investigate further. He was accustomed to the shouting but not inured to it and furthermore, the tirade was normally aimed at his father so he wondered who might be the recipient of that particular outburst. He opened the door furtively and inched out to gain better aural access. He could hear the voice of Grace stridently assaulting his sister and as he edged up those first four steps and popped his head around the corner, he could see Martha's shape in the doorway of the bedroom that Michelle and Grace shared. Grace's voice was still screeching and Danny felt a wave of fear surge though his body. He was a timid child, placid and not warrior like in his disposition. And even had he been possessed of such traits, he was only nine years old. As the noise went on, he became aware of his sister's voice intermittently respond in some forlorn and whimpering attempt to fight back but she was totally overwhelmed and no possible match for the relentless vocal abuse that was being hurled at her by Grace with an occasional, congruent contribution from Martha.

He didn't know what to do; his heart was beating so ferociously that it felt like it was going to burst out from within his chest. He couldn't leave his sister alone but he was so very scared. If only his father had been home. He wouldn't have let this happen. As the shouting continued without pause, he steeled himself and displaying an audacity that was intrinsically lacking to him, walked up the stairs. Martha was the first to espy his arrival.

'You don't need to be up here,' she said.

'I want to be with my sister,' he replied, not knowing where he was finding the courage to utter the words. With that, he nimbly skirted around her and entered the room where, to the right, was Michelle, seated on one of the beds against the wall with Grace hovering in intimidating pose above her. His aunt Grace looked at him and he her as he ducked by her and sat to his sister's left between her and the aunts and the door.

Grace was breathing heavily, face reddened with seething, boiling anger. Her shoulders were visibly pulsating and she looked as though she would erupt at any moment. Michelle on the other hand, was sitting next to him, head flat in her hands with her elbows tight to her stomach; it was as though she thought that if she couldn't see them, they wouldn't be able to see her. And she was crying. Without thinking, he placed his arm around her and defiantly looked at Grace. The torrent continued but now he too was party to the invective. He didn't know who was saying what but he made out the odd, 'Why did you ever have to come here?' followed by a 'My mother would still be here had you not moved in,' and more of the same. Michelle had temporarily lost her derring-do, it had been suffocated, dismantled by this adult assault on two vulnerable, powerless children. He, age notwithstanding, did not lose sight of some youthful reason and the only words he uttered were to his sister.

'Don't worry,' he soothed. 'Just try to ignore it. Daddy will be home soon,' and then in a voice slightly more audible intended for more ears than just his sister's, 'We will tell him all about this and then we'll see'. Naturally, this provoked more frenetic, maniacal outbursts from Grace.

He would later wonder how she was able to restrain herself from striking out physically, she was that out of control, at that moment completely awash with hatred and pent up frustration. What sane, adult human being would treat children thus? It was nothing short of miraculous that violence wasn't employed against the two. The verbal onslaught continued however, and now and then Danny, disregarding his own counsel to his sister, would say something, some childish retort, some juvenile attempt at striking back. But he was aware of a growing need to urinate. He was struggling to resist it but the urge was almost irrepressible . He knew he wouldn't be able to hold out for much longer but he really didn't like the idea of abandoning his position as he was unsure if he would be able to reclaim it. He couldn't wet himself; he just couldn't. Finally, he squeezed his sister.

'I have to go and pee,' he explained, 'but I'll come back.' She nodded and he stood and walked past the harridans and went down the stairs to the toilet.

'That's right,' said Grace, 'you go to bed now. You always go to bed at this time, no need for you to be here.' Whilst in midflow, he was aware of Grace's footsteps echoing down the same stairs and stop right outside the door.

He had finished his discharging but didn't pull the chain, thinking that she might think he was engaged in more than just a pee and perhaps she would get bored and go away. She didn't. He was really nervous now. It was one thing trying to be brave and tough in company with his sister, it was something altogether different by himself against Grace at night by those stairs. His earlier out of character boldness had dissolved.

His heart was racing again, not helped by her lack of utterances from outside the toilet, such silence only lending weight to his dark imaginings. Finally, he knew he had to emerge. It wasn't only fear for himself he felt but also a burning desperation not to leave his sister all alone against these relentless women. He knew he was a weak little boy and he knew that his aunt was aware that he didn't possess the same bravado persona that was usually the province of his sister. Grace was the adult and he was a compliant, obedient little boy. He did as he was told under normal circumstances. But these were anything other than normal circumstances.

He turned back to the seat of the toilet giving it a cursory glance, pulled the chain and exited hoping that maybe he hadn't heard her go. She had gone but only to the bottom of the last four steps to the basement, a few metres away.

'Time for you to go to bed,' she repeated from earlier. 'You always go to bed at this hour, so no reason not to tonight.' She was approaching him; he could feel the final threads of his resistance melting away, he knew he was on the verge of capitulation but he thought back to his sister and the tirade she would suffer alone, all by herself with no shield to deflect the caustic ranting. From somewhere, from some instinctive survival strand, from some residual rebellious sentiment, came the words.

'I'm not GOING to bed until my daddy gets back!'

'Yes, you are!' she screamed.

'YOU COW!!' he bellowed, blood rushing, sinews stiff.

She was palpably shocked to hear such unexpected language from the timid child and it threw her off balance momentarily, at which point he seized his opportunity, ran back up the stairs, past Martha and re-took his earlier position. Grace was hot on his heels and resumed the diatribe. This time the two children stayed quiet, letting it flow over them as tempting as it was to react, desperate for it to stop. Danny had his arm about his sister as before but there was one more last comment he would make which would stay with him forever not just for its content but for the unmistakable effect it had on Martha.

'You shouldn't be here, this isn't your home,' she said. Danny turned to face her, his eyes now sodden and moist as those two children sat next to each other, helpless but together.

'We don't like it either, BUT IT'S THE ONLY HOME WE'VE GOT LEFT!' he cried. Martha's hand sped to her face as tears instantly engulfed her and she turned and left the room sobbing and perhaps coming to her senses, shocked at her own level of bullying. The screaming died down. The noise abated. Grace was still trying to cajole or manipulate Danny into going to bed but he was going nowhere.

They had no idea what time it was when they finally heard the key in the front door but they knew it was their father; they were up and at his side in a flash, one at either flank, clutching a respective leg.

'Can't we leave here, Daddy, please?! Can't we go back to Cressy Road or to Aunty Winnie?? Please, Daddy, pleaseeee.'

And he, immediately aware that something terrible had transpired, said plaintively, 'Oh no, what's happened now??'

~~~~~~~~~~~~~~~~~~~~~~~~

WINNIE

Winnie was his mother's sister, another aunt. But this was a nice aunt; an extremely nice aunt. She had four children of her own, his cousins, Michelle's cousins. Aileen, Gary, Sally and Tracy. Tracy was the youngest and although he was closer to Sally's age with whom he got on extremely well, his favourite was Tracy. Winnie's husband, Arthur, was a delightful man too. He once told the young ones off but in a way that did not inspire terror nor lasting fear. It was *norma** telling off.

In the Cressy Road era, those halcyon days that would end all too soon, he and his sister spent much time with Winnie's family, particularly Sally and Tracy as the other two were much older and many times, Aileen would adopt more of a supervisory capacity than playmate figure. They were true Londoners, salt of the earth, he would never have any recollection of them other than fond and loving.

The only house of theirs that he could remember was a tall, town house kind of affair, in Islington coincidentally, Again, his memories of this were and would remain cherished and warm, much like the atmosphere of the abode itself. Comfortable and homely, all so different from the stark, decrepit Gerrard Road equivalent. Perhaps it wasn't just the physical entity that wrought such a pronounced contrast so much as the people who resided in the respective interiors.

There weren't that many specific memories but that's unsurprising since the timeline of association was limited almost exclusively to the first seven years of his life and of that, the first two could be reasonably eliminated as not memorable and the last two were occupied by more urgent and pressing matters.

Nonetheless, he remembered travelling on buses, upstairs if seats available, sometimes bickering but the *normal* type of bickering between young children, nothing with lasting recriminations, he remembered cinema excursions and he remembered the house. He simply remembered liking being with them very much.

This existing status quo changed radically following the death of his mother. It was a total polar reversal. The family he barely knew, on his father's side suddenly became the key familial element, in fact the *only* familial presence in his life and the family that he had known for most of his conscious life up until his seventh year were clinically excised from his existence.

There is no doubt he was a very young child and could not have any concept of the demands of raising children, financially as well as the whole compass of exigent requirements and duties involved. Unaware he may have been of such logistics and perhaps this was why he and his sister were not absorbed within that tight family structure of which Winnie was the architect but he did not believe then and he certainly never believed later that there would not have at least taken place a dialogue about the possibility of such an assimilation.

It would have been an arduous task of disproportionate difficulty but he did not doubt for a second, not a one, that an offer, some compromise, some working around the edges, would have been suggested by his mother's sister.

What he believed more was that some Machiavellian scheming had been afoot that deliberately excluded the Winnie tribe from the proceedings. Maybe some inter family rivalry, some obsession with inner-directed privacy, some desire to claim full proprietary rights influenced the outcome but what could absolutely *not* be doubted was that the interests of Danny and his sister were consigned to the bottom of the heap.

The chronology of some events were a little hazy in those inchoate days but he did recall one occasion when he had been told that Winnie and his cousins were coming that evening to take him and his sister to the pictures. The joyous expectation that he felt about their visit and imminent evening out was a measure of the abiding closeness which itself implied that this visit was due to take place soon after the events of Cressy Road. Those bonds forged over seven years were still at that point sturdy and robust and seemed unbreakable.

When the hour was approaching, finding it difficult to contain his excitement, he took up position near the top step of the flight of stairs that led from the toilet to the ground floor passageway which led to the front door.

He had discovered that sitting in a specific spot on specific step on those stairs would allow visual access to the small gap between the door and the floor which would reveal approaching feet some seconds before a knock heralded their official arrival. He had come to discover this particular step because this step had more than one purpose. On many an early, summer evening, he would sit in this very spot, hoping for and willing the onset of the heavy sounding thud of Philip's unmistakable footsteps followed by the measured version of Charlie's own as this was often the antecedent of a jaunt to Hackney Marshes where an hour or so would be joyously spent in all consuming football mania. It was marginally better when Martin came too as then there would then be enough players for a goalkeeper as Charlie's lungs, heavy with smoke, did not permit him more than one or two minutes of exertion.

More often than not alas, the incipient steps of his cousin did not venture past their owner's bedroom and after a painstaking vigil, Danny would re-trace his steps downstairs as the fading of the light clearly mirrored the fading of hope of a football indulgence.

This occasion was different because of its total uniqueness. Tracy and Sally, such frequent companions and comrades for so long, didn't come to call anymore. Such irony was that given the greater ease in travel terms from his cousins' home to Gerrard Road which was a walk compared to a tube trip when they were Cressy Road visitors. He imagined the things they would likely do that evening and supposed that it would be similar to all those previous outings, probably a bus involved, jostling for the seat by the window or at the front of the vehicle, preferably aloft, some sweets, choosing who would take which seat where inside the cinema and so on..

Michelle didn't seem as enthused by the idea or perhaps was more sanguine despite her youth but whichever reason, she wasn't perched by his side in fervid anticipation. But every time he heard a footstep or voice outside in the street, he brought his gaze fixedly to that gap and willed it to be the voice or foot belonging to the hoped for body that would turn to approach the door.

He didn't know how long he had waited before he went downstairs to enquire if anyone knew anything. He hadn't heard the telephone so he knew that no-one had rung to advise of a late arrival.

'Where are they?' he asked Grace. 'They should be here by now, shouldn't they?'

'I don't know,' she said in an insouciant manner. He returned to his observation post. Michelle came up some time later and announced matter of factly,

' They aren't comin', Dan.'

'How do you know?' he rejoined.

'Coz they'd be here by now,' she said with little emotion.

'They'll come,' he said stubbornly and returned his line of vision to the gap.

'Ok,' she said with a shrug and went back down to the basement. When the light began to fade, just as with Hackney Marshes, he knew they weren't coming.

Not because it was dark, which would be the sole impediment to football engagement but because they were *so* late, they would definitely have at least phoned to give some advance notice of their tardiness. Even though he was certain they would not be coming now, as he went back down the stairs, resigned to the fact and to his disappointment, a tiny spark of hope remained and his descent took much longer than the distance merited since he would stop at every stair to look back to that gap, and as he neared the bottom, he had to stand on tip toe to look over the top to get one more look.

When later in life he thought back over events of that time, he would try to employ an adult's rationale rather than use a child's perspective. Of that particular event, he was sure, positive, that it was not an act of wilful intent on Winnie's part that prevented the rendezvous that evening. He was much more inclined towards the likelihood that the forces that stoked the fires of Gerrard Road were responsible and had proffered some flaccid excuse or reason to Winnie as to why her trip would prove redundant and not worth pursuing. Perhaps as an adult he was viewing the past through nostalgic tinted glasses but if conclusions can be drawn from observable reality and historical trends, then his inclination was more likely correct.

Moreover, his father could not be discharged from some level of complicity or responsibility in the fragmentation of what had been an established relationship between his children and those of his dead wife's sister, even if it were passive in nature. And indeed, as much as he loved his father and love him he did, this would not be the first time that he would have cause to question his father's behaviour and inactivity.

Some years later, when Danny was about fourteen years old, maybe fifteen but certainly that age when swagger and swelling arrogance began to surface in the adolescent, and when those infrangible, unbreakable bonds between him and his mother's family had long since been broken and splintered asunder, Winnie came to call at Christmas time. To his knowledge, this was the first time he had seen her and she him and his sister since the early days of those life changing events.

He and Philip and some others were in the living room. Danny was at the age when he sought to impress other boys by his prowess and daring and comedic cleverness and suddenly an unexpected opportunity presented itself to impress Philip with his comedy genius. Winnie entered with a smile so obviously genuine, depicting the level of delight that she was so clearly experiencing in seeing her only nephew for the first time in many years. He was standing at the far side of the room with Philip beside him.

She approached, leaned forward to touch his arm and kiss him, and then, with her other arm, presented to him a neatly wrapped gift. She stood there before him, keenly observing as he unwrapped it carelessly, and then removing the contents -it was a jumper, a beautiful garment- he held it aloft before him and cruelly, with a voice laden with undisguised, heavy sarcasm said loudly enough to impress his cousin, indifferent to the loving aunt who was so very pleased to see him, indifferent to whatever malign force had for so many years prevented her from seeing her niece and nephew,

'Oh, just what I alwaaaays wanted.'

His sardonic sneering was unmistakable but she pretended not to have noticed it. The beaming smile never left her face, she didn't wince, she didn't even blink at the scathing wound that his callous words had inflicted. She revealed none of the disappointment that she at that moment felt, the sadness at the wasted years, the loss of love like water running through partially cupped hands.

He stood there, feeling big and clever in front of his cousin, totally insensitive to the abject and inconsolable upset that his puerile but coldhearted behaviour had caused her. He was already becoming a product of his mother's death, insular and detached from emotion. Determined to be self sufficient, reliant on no-one; but what terrible, emotional cost. He wasn't the only victim of his mother's death. His aunt Winnie, his mother's only sister, died in 1984, about nine years later. But after that Christmas, he would never see his loving aunt again.

~~~~~~~~~~~~~~~~~~~~~~

THE CHURCH INCIDENT

Following that first initial eruption which so brutally swamped and burnt two young children with its scalding lava of unrestrained abuse, there was a period of less fraught existence. Grace's emptied sacks of venom and pent up frustration had to be fully replenished before bursting point was reached once more. Martha's self-removal as an active protagonist almost certainly contributed to the lull. It seemed that his final words had penetrated the temporary fog of her loss of reason and brought realisation that this type of unwarranted assault on two harmless and innocuous children was simply unacceptable. She, to his recollection, although never occupying a place of significant importance nor affection in his heart after that display of antipathy, never again exhibited the same nefarious and contemptible behaviour. She did often adopt the role of observer though, being present when Grace would scream and hurl her toxic detritus but often, the row would turn in on itself and back out in an alternate direction in which Martha would sometimes find herself the object of Grace's limitless virulence, his father too, on one side or the other. Had it not been so grievous and abhorrent to witness at the time, it would have been funny. All comers and free for alls. Rows that had probably been going on between these siblings from their own earliest days of childhood. The three men who lived upstairs were rarely involved. They had more sense.

The fact was that Martha was not the harridan from hell that Grace was. And even Grace's range of harridan behaviour was largely confined to the environs in which Danny and Michelle existed.

It was always of interest to him in later life that when he relayed to various members of his family some of the events that had occurred in his time at Gerrard, they were genuinely shocked and unaware. Dirty laundry downstairs at Gerrard Road was a private affair from the outset and would remain so throughout.

In any event, the humanity and underlying decency of Martha revealed itself when what started as a one off invitation to Michelle to join her and Charlie, Martin and Philip on their annual British caravanning holiday became an open invitation for most ensuing years. They even went abroad on at least one occasion.

Danny's familial direction and preferred choice lay elsewhere, to Bernard and his family. Bernard was his father's older brother, who had seen active service in World War Two. He was a short, bald man like Danny's father and supremely ambitious unlike Danny's father. He had a wife and two daughters and with these cousins, the little boy would ultimately spend most of his youthful summers, Christmases too; he would have lived with them had he been able. Later on he discovered that that too had actually been an option considered but not exercised. The times that were spent with them were undeniably his best and happiest, the most decent memories that he would take from the grim habitation that was Gerrard Road .

Soon after his mother's death, his father and he went on holiday with them, to Spain. They drove there in a beautiful Jaguar, the old Z Cars type but there was nothing old about it then.

It was Bernard's car but the two brothers shared the driving and although it was the first time Danny had been abroad and although he was with people with whom he loved being, the holiday was equally memorable for the amount of alcohol his father consumed.

He rarely ventured out with them during the day as he was normally sound asleep, anesthetised by the brown liquid that as the years gathered momentum would have an ever increasing presence. That was the first time Danny had seen his father indulge to that extent his propensity for whisky.

There was a good deal of singing in the car too, to distract from the tedium of the endless road unfurling mile after mile, to distract from the increasing temperature as they neared warmer climes. His aunt, Bernard's wife was of Italian extraction and had an operatic voice; her voice possessed a formidable and seductive allure. She was an amateur but amateur in terms of payment, not ability. She sang at weddings now and then; his own mother was an operatic singer too. She also sang at weddings and various engagements and he was led to understand that she was paid for it. Bernard's wife always insisted that Danny's mother was a superior singer to her; his mother had actually appeared on Opportunity Knocks when it was a radio presentation and had come second, beaten by a populist comedian. She had even cut a vinyl record of herself in Selfridges, singing *Ave Maria* which he had heard as Michelle would later manage to gain possession of a crackly and degenerating copy preserved for modern day consumption.

Danny and Michelle appeared to have inherited these euphonic voices and mellifluous tones, and even his father was possessed of a rich, baritone organ.

On the occasions when his mother and father and he and Michelle would attend church on a Sunday morning which served as the vehicle for his mother's principal broadcast by way of the church choir, he would also hear his father's tones emerge and drift off on a melodic cloud of sound. One Sunday, on such an occasion, they were all getting ready to go.

'Hurry up, Danny!' said his father. 'We will be late!'

'I have to pee, Dad!' he called back, heading to the toilet.

'Well, hurry up. Your mother has to sing.'

He entered the loo, and holding his jumper and shirt up with his chin tucked down trapping the two articles against his upper chest, pulled down his zip and peed trying to make circles and squares from different coloured liquids as the cascade merged with the dormant waters below.

'HURRY UP!' Startled and returning to reality, he hurriedly squeezed his bits back in, pulled up his zip and pulling the chain by the attached string which allowed little people to remove the evidence of their ablutions, ran out to his family who were impatiently waiting.

They went down the stairs leading to the front door, jumped in the car and set off on the short journey to the church and mass. It was an early Sunday morning and the city still lay in quiet and languid slumber. The two children were in the back with Michelle gazing idly out of the window at the passing shapes and colours in some autonomous reverie.

His father was half focused on the vacant road as he guided his Ford with nonchalant ease, whilst his mother was rapt in her own independent thoughts. The little boy was fully conscious however, but not focused on the outer street nor immersed in some inventive fantasy. He was focused on his nether regions.

They arrived at the Catholic church and upon entering, his mother scaled the stairs to the balcony area which was the domain of the choir and her seat of sovereign whilst the other three went aloft to the balcony adjacent. They sat on an available pew with his father sitting in between him and Michelle. The service began and the abundant congregation stood to acknowledge the priest's presence. Danny stood too but his mind was not on the priest, the congregation nor any other feature of that Sunday morning mass, his mind was firmly in his pants which seemed to be biting his dinky with his every movement. He tried moving to his left to see if the same sensation was elicited, then to his right but no matter which way he moved, the mordant feeling followed him. He slipped his hand down the front of his trousers trying to be as inconspicuous as possible in an attempt to move the pants away from his bits and thereby bring an end to this increasingly unpleasant feeling.

'Danny!!' loudly whispered his father close to his ear. 'Stop fidgeting and take your hands out of your trousers immediately!!'

'But Daddy, it hurts!'

'Shhh.' The audience took their seats as the priest initiated the service and Danny was feeling more and more uncomfortable.

It was as though something like barbed glue was sticking to his dinky. Every time he moved a leg, even slightly, it pulled on his trousers which in turn pulled on whatever was causing the discomfort.

The faithful stood again for the first hymn and beneath the lofty soprano of his mother, he could make out the deeper tones of his father beside him. He tugged at his sleeve, pulling downwards to get his father to his height. On tiptoe, the unpleasant feeling increased. His father shrugged his son's arm off with as little overtness as possible. Danny persisted.

'Dad,' he whispered loudly, 'DAD!'. His father finally bent down, conscious of surrounding eyes upon him and said,

'ENOUGH! We are at mass! BEHAVE yourself and tell me after.'

'But Dad, it really hurts!'

'What hurts?' Danny beckoned him closer and then in spite of the pain, stood on tiptoe and almost touching his father's inner ear with his lips, whispered as gently as he could,

'My *dinky*!'

His father re-assumed an upright position and looked down at his son who was looking back at him with intermittently squinting eye whilst practically hopping from foot to foot trying to shake off the uncomfortable sensation. His father realised his son was in some difficulty so pointing to the end of the pew, he gestured to him to go.

He quickly whispered to his daughter telling her he was going outside for a moment and not to leave without her mother or himself. She nodded her obedience and he followed his son down the stairs and out of the church.

'OK,' he said, 'tell me what's the matter with you.'

'It's my dinky, Daddy, it's stuck to something,' he explained.

'What do you mean *stuck to something*? Stuck to what?'

'I don't know Daddy, but it's following me wherever I move.'

'Alright,' said his father, 'let's find somewhere quiet and we can take a look.' They moved a little way from the church and came to a quiet road with a bin attached to a wall and placing his son by the bin with the wall behind and himself in front so as to prevent any casual observer's view as best he could, he told the boy to take his trousers down and see what had happened. The little boy started to unzip his trousers when unexpectedly he yelped in pain.

'What is it?' asked his startled father.

'It's stuck Daddy, it's stuck!' said the boy, quickly becoming agitated.

'What's stuck??' asked the father with a concerned tone, aware now that this was a rapidly emerging crisis.

'My dinky!!' cried the son.

'Yes, but *what's* it stuck too?' said the father, increasingly anxious himself.

'To my zip!'

'OK,' said his father, adopting calmer tones to prevent panic gaining ascendancy.

'Let me look.' His son complied and turning to face his father, indicated the zip that had somehow captured within its teeth the foreskin close to the head of his penis, much like a fox carrying in its teeth its prey by the neck.

'What are we going to do, Daddy??' The man didn't answer, he was examining the scene and trying to think of the most effective way to detach the predatory zip from the little boy's ensnared dinky. He was at a complete loss.

'I can't take my trousers off, Daddy, because they will pull my dinky off with them. What happens when I want to pee, Daddy?' His father was still focused on the predicament before him. 'How will I be able to go to school, Daddy?' he was really beginning to panic now as a whole range of dark and worrisome thoughts flooded in.

'I'm going to try and gently pull the zip down, Danny. I'll be as gentle as I can.'

'OK, Dad.' But before the man had even taken hold of the zip, the boy winced and drew back as though he had been touched with a red hot poker.

'I haven't even touched the zip yet!' lamented his father. 'Stand still.' The boy straightened himself and his father once more prepared for the delicate manoeuvre. Once more he recoiled as soon as he felt his father's presence. 'Danny! You are going to have to let me touch the zip.'

'Alright, Daddy, but it hurts!'

'I haven't even touched you yet!!' complained the grown up.

Heaven knows what any passer by seeing a grown man kneeling down in front of a young child whose trousers were slightly loosened and hanging down as far as the unyielding zip would allow would have been thinking. The reality was that a loving father was increasingly disconsolate at his inability to remove the source of his only son's pain and anguish. Finally, he managed to take hold of the zip.

'Right, I'm going to start moving the zip down, Danny. Keep still.' His son nodded, holding his breath, scared to move or to antagonise that nasty zip in any way. His father began to pull the zip but he was so gentle, it was like stroking a suppurating wound. The boy cried out plaintively and his father realised he was not equipped for this task.

By now, the throng had begun to emerge from their place of worship, liberated from duty and ready to enjoy the rest of the day with clear conscience.

'Wait here a minute, Danny. I'm just going to tell Mum what's happened and then I'll be back.' The boy murmured an ok and off went his father. He could see him animatedly talking to his mother who had Michelle by her side. His sister kept throwing inquisitive glances over to him but he looked away and kept his hands strategically over his trousers even though there was nothing to see.

'Ok, Danny. Your mother and sister are going to walk home and we are going to the hospital,' declared his father, more relaxed and confident again now that he would be enlisting professional assistance and had formulated a firm stratagem.

'Hospital??' cried the boy, now for the first time in the initial throes of tears. 'But I don't want to go to the hospital, Daddy! They will cut my dinky off. PLEASE don't let's go to the hospital! I will stay still this time, honest. You do it. Daddy, PLEASEEEE!' He was mildly hysterical.

'Don't be silly, Son, of course they wont cut it off!' said his father but not so re-assuring that his son felt less concerned.

'But how do you know they won't, Daddy?? How else will they untangle my dinky?'

'They are doctors, Danny. I promise you they won't cut your dinky off!' The boy went quiet and remained so as they drove to the hospital on what had started as such a quiet and uneventful day of rest.

At the hospital, they made to their way to the A & E department and his father told him to sit and wait while he went to the counter to brief the receptionist on what had happened. When he returned, he sat next to his boy and they waited some while until a nurse approached them and bade them to follow her to a small cubicle walled by an extendable curtain. Danny was sitting on a gurney with his father in the chair beside him, neither saying anything. Danny's hand hovered continuously over the afflicted area as though a protective mantle.

After some while, the curtain flicked back and there before them was a young, dark haired man in a white coat, presumably the doctor. Danny warmed to his manner immediately.

'So,' he said,' I understand a young man has had his private parts ambushed by a zip!' Danny liked the expression *private parts*, it was more grown up than dinky and he also liked the idea that it was like a battleground and he had been ambushed by the enemy. However, he didn't like the discomfort that continued to endure nor not knowing what the doctor intended to do about it.

'And you are Danny, are you not?' he said smiling in such a mollifying way that Danny was completely disarmed. He nodded.

'Yes, he is Danny,' volunteered his father. The doctor looked at his father conspiratorially.

'OK, sir, ok with you that I have a quick gander?'

'Certainly, Doctor,' said the father, secretly relieved that he could now delegate his son's well being to a much more qualified individual.

'Splendid.' He pulled up a chair and sat right in front of Danny, legs wide to enable close access to the boy.

'How old are you, Danny?'

'I'm six,' he said, 'almost seven!'

'Excellent! You are a big boy!' The lad smiled. This doctor really did have outstanding people skills.

'So, I'm just going to take a look to see what we are dealing with, ok with you?' The boy nodded. 'Could you hold your shirt and jumper up for me please?' Without answering, Danny raised the garments and secured them with his chin as he had done earlier that morning.

The doctor lowered his head and looked down at the area that was creating the drama. He skirted the trousers and the zip with his fingers and looked up when Danny flinched without cause other than imagination. The doctor looked up at him and drawing back said,

'So, Danny, what's your favourite toy?' and while he was waiting for the answer, continued with his visual examination.

'Ummm, my best toy is…,' before he had time to answer but adequately distracted, the doctor had grabbed the zip and yanked it down with the speed of a bullet. Danny's private part fell loose, free of its shackle although slightly sore.

'There. All done!' said the doctor. Danny looked down at his private part, he was slightly in shock. There it was dangling, free but still attached to his body, and not a drop of blood. Relief surged over him.

'Sometimes speed is all you need, like removing a plaster,' said the doctor to Danny's equally relieved father, winking as he did so.

'Thank you,' said his dad. 'Say thank you, Danny.'

'Thank you.'

'My pleasure, young man, just be more careful where you put your dinky next time,' he said chuckling.

They drove back to Cressy Road, drama diffused and went indoors where his mother and sister were engaged in their normal Sunday activities. What a story this would make for school playtime tomorrow. Danny, the hero of the Battle of the Zip…

~~~~~~~~~~~~~~~~~~~~~~~

HIS DAD

His dad was a lovely, gentle and congenial man. An average chap. Husband, father, son. The events that overtook him however, weren't particularly average. This was not to suggest that they were unique, simply that they weren't commonplace. He had undertaken various jobs throughout his life, never really settling in one until his most recent with the London Underground. Perhaps it was the intrinsic shiftwork that preserved his interest in that specific labour since the regular changes in work patterns may have satisfied some innate craving for new experiences or mitigated his reluctance to commit fully to Sisyphean doctrine. A kind of half way house.

At one time, in the nineteen fifties, he had joined his older siblings, Bernard and Grace, in a cottage industry from set up in Gerrard Road which manufactured optical frames. All the other siblings at some point had a measure of involvement in the business too, but to what extent, the boy would never know. It didn't matter. They worked out of the kitchen in the basement where Danny spent so much of his young life. Although the kitchen on the surface seemed as one room, actually it was both a kichen *and* a scullery and on close inspection, the fact that it had been demarcated at one point was obvious. There still remained a divide raised an inch or so, no obstacle to speak off, a slightly raised bump between the two. The scullery may well have been an extension although given its crude nature, neither an expensive nor very professional one.

This addendum which was at the far end of the kitchen, contained a door to the garden (yard really, with some grass for lip service to more ambitious aspirations) and when you were inside it, the scullery, the differences between it and the rest of the kitchen were self-evident. The wall at the back was fully exposed, revealing the naked bricks but not ornate and pretty bricks contrived for aesthetic effect. They were proper functional bricks with all the wear and tear that such functionality exposed for purpose undergo, shabby, ragged asymmetrical types, grubby and unclean . There were spiders and woodlice aplenty as well as abundant dirt in undisguised view and overall a general impression of questionable hygiene and visible squalour.

The floor was covered in disparate pieces of lino, thrown down with little care or interest, and lay where they had fallen, no semblance of uniformity nor colour consistency, gaps wherein the underlying floor was visibly apparent here and there. The ceiling was mostly constructed of some frosted perspex with strands of deserted cobwebs, like billowing, silky stalactites, hanging down from the only non translucent parts of the roof that flanked the central perspexed theme and when it rained it was always a matter of amazement that that perspex did not collapse under the force of the precipitation seeking domininion upon it. Though it *definitely* leaked..

There were also some relics of the business that had once been plied with such hopeful optimism from that tiny backwater. An ancient cupboard, useless, ugly old thing still sat in indolent silence, housing all manner of eclectic tools that only saw the light of day when Danny used to peer inside its innards seeking toy potential but finding none.

A solitary vice lingered, at the back, atop the cupboard, rusting and discarded, purpose long since past, a small, delicate screwdriver, unwanted and forsaken, its only company. The scullery's sole use after the business had long since failed and closed was for the sink that found itself opposite the wall described, itself lodged against a similar wall with an odd interspersal of tiles interrupting the bleak range of undecorated and cracked dark brick. A cold water tap dangled down and some sort of boiler mechanism, small volume, the source of the hot liquid was at the other end of the sink. This was where they washed, those lower residents, this was where the majority of their ablutions took place.

Danny would clean his teeth here and in the midst of the brushing motion, observe the fearless, peripatetic lice moving in and out of small cracks and indentations in the brick façade in front of him. He never dared venture his hand in whatever living horror inhabited the regions below the basin. Eventually, he would assume it was normal.

This was the home that his father had deserted when he had met and married that woman so ill fated from birth. Like a bird fleeing the nest, off to build a life and family of his own, full of dreams, full of love, full of hope. That was the home to which he returned when those dreams were dashed on the rocks of callous whim, shipwrecked on the shores of cruel fate, demolished with scant regard to their architect. This was not part of the plan.

The nature of his father's job afforded perhaps the only beneficial side effect of the whole calamity, the ability to change location with minimal difficulty and to edit shift patterns.

This was of particular significance following that first shocking exhibition of malevolence. After that, his father did not feel comfortable leaving his children alone at night. For this reason, and for the sake of convenience for its own sake, he succeeded in effecting a transfer from Hampstead to Highbury and Islington tube which was and is on the Victoria line and only a hop away on the bus. It was even close enough to walk if necessary.

As well as changing place of work, Danny's father also began avoiding late shifts as much as he was able to ensure that his presence at home coincided with that of his children. As they were at school most of the day and as Grace worked from nine til around five every weekday, the evenings were by far the most vulnerable periods. His father's manipulation of his working roster were very successful in limiting the time of exposure that would pose the greatest threat to his children and he also knew that of course, they wouldn't be young, defenceless and toothless pups forever.

There were few memories of play and outings with his father. The midnight feast was one of course, another was going to the Science Museum in Kensington. They would have gone naturally by the underground, probably the Northern line from the Angel to King's Cross and then change onto the Piccadilly and travel direct to South Kensington. Many of the London museums were and are congregated in the same area and served by the same station but they only went to the one from his recollection.

He remembered sitting in the smoking car of the train (how extraordinary to consider there actually used to exist one entire car dedicated to the smoking fraternity on the London Underground), looking around the tube whilst his father was smoking his frequently present non tipped Player cigarette. He was reading the Sun, he always read the Sun unless he wanted a more challenging crossword puzzle, then he would elect the Daily Telegraph. As a point of reference, the Sun's crossword was and remains an excellent entry and self-teaching aid for the domain of cryptic puzzles since it offers two sets of clues for the same answer, one cryptic, one not. This is the device his father used to teach his son.

It was not the museum itself that earmarked that day but one of the passengers in the same car sitting almost opposite the father and son. Danny's eyes had fallen upon him after a survey of the posters decorating the sides of the train, one of which eulogised a band who sounded like a question about a deaf, dumb and mute child and another speaking of coloured balls being pocketed on black and white TV; what caught the boy's attention was the man's stare. He wasn't staring at the boy, although he was clearly conscious of the boy staring at him. It was the eyes. There was something about those eyes, bulbous and crooked that seemed very familiar. Danny continued to stare at the man who was still avoiding his gaze.

'Daddy,' he whispered as he raised himself to his father's ear, never taking his eyes off the man. Those eyes were mesmerising. 'Daddy!' he whispered more loudly, competing against the rocking rumbling of the train.

'What, Danny?' his father said, leaning slightly toward him but still intent on whatever article was currently under his scrutiny.

'Can you ask that man for his signature?' he said.

'In a minute,' replied his unfocused father, not really hearing what his son was asking.

'But Daddy, he may get off at the next stop!' No answer. Perhaps the outbreak of violence in a troubled Ireland or Manchester City vanquishing Leicester to lift a cup aloft held more interest for him.

'Daddy!!' the boy persisted, pulling at his father's arm and now looking at him, 'Please ask him.' His father, now alert to his son's strange request, interrupted his perusal.

'Who, Danny?' he asked, looking around the carriage. 'What are you talking about?' Within seconds his father knew whom he meant and the man opposite conscious of being the topic of the father-son dialogue, turned and smiled at the father. His dad smiled back and said,

'You ask him, Danny. He wont bite.' The man turned his gaze, his trademark stare away from the father to the boy and smiled. Danny pulled himself into his fathers shoulder, demure and coy.

'But I'm shy, Daddy,' he said, addressing his father but watching the man.

'Go on, don't be shy, he may get out before you get a chance as you said,' and he tore a piece of the least inked paper from the Sun he could find and offered it to his son as he eased a pen from the top pocket of his jacket at the same time.

Danny took the offerings and sliding himself tentatively from his seat, he made the one step journey to the man opposite and extending the paper and pen to him said in a hushed voice,

'Could I have your autograph, please?' staggering slightly as the train hobbled unevenly along the track.

'Of course you can,' said the smiling man who was almost certainly looking at the boy as he spoke but his crooked eyes conveying the impression that he was looking at some spot above the lad's head. 'I think I heard your name as Danny?'

'Yes, it's Danny ,' he replied, as the train thundered from darkness into the illumination of the next station, fighting against the irresistible pressure of the brake.

'There you are,' said the man, as he passed the pen and paper back to the waiting boy. 'Cheerio,' he said, as he stood and exited the opened doors.

'Thank you,' called Danny to the wide eyed man's retreating back. Danny turned back to his father, face alive with the excitement of obtaining proof he had met a celebrity. His father smiled back at him.

'Well, what did he write?' he asked. And as the boy reclaimed his seat, now deliberating scouring the train for more celebrity signatures, his father read out loud,

'To Danny, happy travels, your train pal, Marty Feldman.'

As well as the museum, his father once took him to HMS Belfast by Tower Bridge although London Bridge was almost as close. He loved that warship; it was grown up war stuff, a long way from the two fingered guns of the playground as he imagined naval engagements in which he, the heroic captain, would lead his equally heroic crew in pursuit of submerged submarines and launch those depth charges that he had been assured by Charlie were much larger than footballs when enthralling him with his real life tales of dark, maritime days of only three decades before.

He would not return to HMS Belfast until another three decades had elapsed when he took his own son there and which they, he and his own son, together would then re-visit four more times within the space of two years. The grandson that his mother nor his father would ever know.

On another occasion, he recalled his dad taking him and Michelle to the park at the top of Gerrard Road, a park still very much extant and in evidence which had embedded at small intervals in its short one hundred metre length, rocks that came up to the knees of the young boy and at the time seemed like small mountains and ideal for darting in and out at speed.

His father chased him through that craggy terrain but the boy was small and quick and more mobile through that rocky landscape than the adult male and he would speak to himself as he dodged his father, nimbly avoiding his clasp.

'Up here,' he would order himself like a self-directing onboard guidance system, 'through there, between those, over that,' while in the background he could hear his father inches behind him, who could not negotiate the jutting of the rocks and their proturberance with the same dexterity as his son's agility, laughing and spluttering at the same time saying,

'Come here, you little bugger!' and his son would end the pursuit proud to have been victorious against the grown up who had ultimately surrendered to fatigue.

His father seemed to have more free time after his wife had gone. The shift work made this all the more pronounced. So when he was on early turn, being at the station to greet the earliest of the itinerant London commuters, by one pm he was home with the day stretching out before him with little to do. Hence his occasional solitary trips to the cinema; he was bored.

He had few friends, in fact the only one that was consistently in evidence through practically the whole history of the post-Cressy Road era was JD. Every Sunday and Monday evening with an unwavering invariability, there would be the customary ring at the doorbell, a bell that barely had the residual strength to issue its alert as it began to falter almost from first sounding, weakened from long use but still standing, and there would be JD who would descend the stairs on the way to the living room, futilely tapping the barometer that bestrode the wall just outside in the hall to assist it provide an accurate reading.

In those few remaining years when his father was still able to walk unaided or at least with minimal assistance, they would normally make their way down to the pub about half a mile away, the Albert. The establishment housed a bar billiard table, a game Danny always thought pointless, a view not shared by the legendary Joe Davis, not to be confused with his father's friend JD. Later, when he was no longer able to walk under his own devices, JD would still keep those weekly appointments at Gerrard and they would share a half bottle of whisky in the room that would become his father's living grave.

Many years later, when Danny was in the throes of his own meltdown, when he was using every mechanism and device suggested by experts to assist him in banishing his own demons, he sought and found JD's number and on one occasion phoned him to thank him for having been his father's only friend who didn't abandon him when no longer able to function on anything other than the most basic of levels. JD was a light on the bleak and wretched wasteland of his father's latter day existence, after Michelle and Danny had fled the coop as soon as they were able, albeit using very different exit strategies, forging their own life paths. JD was the only decent and regular and socially enjoyable communion that his father had in the final years of his life on this earth.

When the rows and arguments at Gerrard had become staple fodder on the menu of their lives and had become simply too constant to endure, whilst his father was still adequately mobile and fully in control of his faculties, there was still hope of creating a better life.

Michelle and Danny used to urge him, *plead* with him to find a flat, to move from that souless home, away from Grace and her manic tirades, so that all three of them, the remaining survivors of Cressy Road, could resume a life together, in normality and loving familial environs and leave that woman alone to rant with herself. They wouldn't even have had confidence going to Winnie or Bernard by this time, so mistrusting had they become of the intentions of anyone other than themselves. The only people they wanted to be with was each other. The three of them. They had been fine before, they could be fine again, albeit it minus one pivotal member.

Their father lacked the nerve to undertake the enterprise. Danny was too young to see how onerous the venture must have appeared to his father but in that youthful, myopic and two dimensional vision that prevented him from seeing the wider logistics involved, he would try to remove the obstacles that were impeding his father's acquiescence to the idea.

'But we *would* be ok, Daddy,' he insisted. 'I could wash up and Michelle could learn to cook. Mrs Tate might be able to come and take us to school again. We could do it, Daddy, we *really* could!'

But his father just didn't have the nerve nor the will and even when Danny persisted with the same plea in his mid-teen years, he knew it was falling on deaf ears and the then present wheelchair would be an even greater obstacle than those previous impediments.

Perhaps his father thought his shift patterns would mean leaving young children alone too often without the wherewithal to look after themselves.

Perhaps he was already aware of a dark cloud building above his health that would eventually burst in an outpouring of further tragedy. Perhaps he just abrogated his responsibility for his own self-interests. Who knows but Danny would never blame him for it. But by the time he was incapacitated for good, the moment had passed and Michelle and Danny would have to inseminate the seeds of their own interests in the hope that they would blossom in a more salubrious harvest.

Had they made the move, things may have been so very different; his father may not have become as ill as he did, Danny and his sister may have had a much more emotionally stable upbringing without becoming so accustomed to hostile and bellicose behaviour and surroundings that in later life they would frequently seek to reproduce, Danny's education may have taken a very different path, his father may have met a woman and re-discovered love in his life... But these things were not meant to be. Gerrard Road was and would remain central to their lives now and for the next decade or so. There was to be no easy release, no saviour to extricate them from that forlorn, cold and dark place. They would have no choice but to be patient.

~~~~~~~~~~~~~~~~~~~~~

GERRARD ROAD (part 2)

It was a combination of factors that made Gerrard Road such
an unwholesome place in which to grow up for Danny and his
sister. First of all, the physical constitution of the building
itself. Cressy Road had been a small flat on the first floor of a
three floored house. The ground floor comprised the first
apartment on entrance to the building and was not self
contained. There was no self-containment for Danny's home
either and for the Gibbons who lived upstairs, access to their
place was gained by walking up the stairs from the front door,
directly through Danny's home and then up the final flight.
The Gibbons' own flat was separated from his by a door that
served as a barrier at the bottom of that final flight. No rooms
of the various flats were ever encroached, it was the stairs and
the various landings of each residence that were subject to
frequent alien trespass although any individual room whose
door was open would be visible to anyone who happened to
be passing

As for the make up of the flat there itself, there was a kitchen
at the top of that first set of stairs which led up from the front
door, then, upon ascending a mini set of three more steps, on
the right was located the bedroom which housed both Danny
and his sister. Directly in front of that small set of steps was
the lounge which had the dual purpose of living room and
bedroom for Danny's parents. In between the practically
adjacent childrens' bedroom and the lounge was the bathroom
of the notorious zip renown.

The flat was small and not ideal in privacy terms but it didn't bother Danny although it almost certainly would have bothered his adult parents who must have seen this as a short term arrangement and who would have progressed to a more appropriate dwelling at some point had fate not engineered a different path.

But small or not, it was a proper home inhabited by a proper family and an aura of security, safety, love and happiness pervaded the place. There were no lice, no dereliction, no visible dirt nor shabbiness. There was a bath, a shower and best of all, no constant fear of heated and fiercely hostile arguments that could erupt at any minute and undermine the whole emotional fabric of the home. This perhaps gives an image of a utopian like existence, an historical chapter viewed through self delusional and rose tinted eyes and prejudiced memory. That is not the case; there were naturally, the invariable arguments that beset families, money related no doubt, differences over minor issues, husband and wife availing themselves of the tacit role of the other to be their partner's emotional punchbag when an offloading was required. But they were *not* the scabrous, brutal, scarring and bitter type that were a regular feature of Gerrard Road. They were not the type that would litter the atmosphere with eggshells for days on end. They were not the type that would linger in the mind and memory forever; they were innocuous and ephemereal, uttered on a whim and carried aloft to the realms of irrelevance soon after their conclusion.

Gerrard Road was everything, absolutely *everything* that Cressy Road was not, its total antithesis. The descriptions espoused thus far probably give the impression of vastness in size but in reality, although the house was home to two relatively independent families, the room number counted only nine. The basement living room and kitchen with the sole toilet four steps up, the two bedrooms on the ground floor, two more of the same on the next floor and the remaining pair of rooms on the top floor. The impression of size emanates from the sprawling nature and stair numeracy of the residence.

What could be said of it without contention however, certainly for the lower regions, was its seedy and shabby interior . The floorboards in many areas were rotting if not rotten and some were positively dangerous. Danny would swear that if you jumped up and down hard enough in Martha's living room, you could end up in bed with the boys below in their bedroom.

Then there were the bannisters or rather, their lack. Staircases resembled old men's toothless smiles; the one leading down to the toilet was particularly prominent in its incomplete array of teeth and when Danny first arrived there, he could fit through the gap at the bottom and bypass those last four steps by jumping down to the basement. As for stabilising effect, those bannisters were like the seductive Sirens of the Hellespont, tempting the climber to enlist their support but ready to collapse under the first meaningful pressure applied.

In addition, hardly any of the doors downstairs closed properly and not one of them closed quietly without some creak or groan revealing their movement.

The carpets were ramshackle and piecemeal. Original material replaced with odd pieces of fabric with God knows what provenance until finally there were different layers building upon different layers until the original was lost to the sight of the disinteresed observer. And here and there lay a tatty rug, colour of no importance, some throw away relic, unwanted by the owner who donated it as a new arrival to the dumping ground of Gerrard Road.

The washing arrangements were, well, at least for Danny, the hardest cross to bear. There was no shower, no bathroom; an old, beaten tin tub, a tiny, tiny vessel in which even at eight, nine and obviously beyond, he would have to sit knees pulled up to his chest to fit. It was stored in a tiny annex -an annex that wasn't really sure if it were part of the inside or the great outdoors- attached to the living room. As patterns and habits began to take shape, Wednesday evenings became the *loosely* designated day for bathtime in the kitchen, that is, if Grace was in a reasonable and not a deliberately obstreperous mood when she would make the boy wait with no seeming good reason, aware of his preoccupation with going to bed at a specific time and his natural inclination to be clean. Sometimes, at the last minute, she would cruelly deny him the right entirely.

On the occasions when he had *permission* to clean himself, he would carry the surprisingly light and manoeuverable tub from annex to kitchen, patiently boil the kettle four times and empty its contents into the vessel, collecting cold water in a bowl whose size demanded three or four trips to the scullery sink and back and then adding it to the steaming content of the tub with careful application to ensure Archimedean principles would not be tested in that kitchen.

Then, drawing the curtain that was furled above that bump which was the demarcation point of scullery and kitchen, he would derobe and delicately insert toe to test the temperature before immersing himself as far as his growing body would allow, hoping that Grace would not begin her badgering for him to finish too soon from outside the door where she would be doubtless hovering.

The whole process from start to finish was comical; really it was. Even attempts to remove soap suds and rinse away their presence was a feat that demanded innovative thinking. A bowl of cold water beside him with a jug to dispense said liquid over his head proved the most efficacious and reliable system. For years he believed it was normal, he was told it was common practice and he believed it despite the absolutely incontrovertible evidence that his own eyes witnessed. Bernard's home wasn't like this, nor was Cressy Road, nor were any of the houses of the other siblings of his father. They had showers, they had baths, bedrooms too, shared or not, in which they could put their own things and not have only a single side of a cupboard allocated for their own use.

Nor was it just his cousins' homes that had such enviable functionality; on the rare visits to a friend's house, there too, he saw true normality. Cleanliness. A shower. How he craved a shower. He would become an above average swimmer but not because he had some clandestine ambition to rival David Wilkie or Mark Spitz so much as a desire to have access to showers and personal hygiene.

Even Martha's place only two floors above was not the bedraggled and threadbare equivalent of downstairs. One possible explanation for this disparity between that lower home and all the others he saw was the nature of its occupancy.

An old woman, Grace the Elder, her full time working spinster daughter and an elderly and insouciant, dapper man who had been the sole dwellers before the migrant arrival, perhaps collectively lacked the resource, the interest or the ability to make a home a home.

The day a few years later when Martha installed a shower up in her kitchen when Michelle optimistically and naievely thought that this would be a benefit open to all, Danny wasn't moved, animated nor hopeful. He knew Martha would never open up the barriers of privacy nor allow a fragmentation of the self containment that was her family which such general access to that most prized of installations would engender. And he was proved right. Glasnost was a west-east entity yet to be realised, there would be no such breaking down of walls north-south in Gerrard.

But the physical structure was only one element of the unpleasantness that made habitation there so unpalatable. That would probably have been bearable, tolerable, had the place not been so loveless and uninviting. Having said that, if the premises had not been so lacking in emotional warmth, then the likelihood is that funds would have been found to make the house a home and a fit environment in which to raise young lives. And when he thought back, it was clear that money must have been available given the combined full time incomes of his father and aunt Grace, the two adults downstairs. It wasn't as if they had profligate or ostentatious life styles; on the contrary, it was a modest existence with no holidays, no expensive luxury. Not even the cost of the housing was high as the family had rented Gerrard Road for over seventy years and had moved onto a protected tenancy which meant low rent, *very* low rent.

There may have been a lack of basic utilities and living standards but there was *never* a dearth of the brown stuff. That was never neglected or underfunded.

The main cause of the lack of warmth and home feeling was Grace. She was unpredictable and capable of spiteful, emotional brutality. While Grace the Elder was alive, she was a very different person but following her mother's death, something changed within her, some seismic shift that unleashed embittered fury that found outlet in the form of vitriol aimed at Danny and his sister and increasingly his father. Her behaviour suggested that she really did blame the little boy and his sister for her own mother's death. The motives didn't much matter to Danny though, as all he saw through those young eyes was a horrible, heinous woman who scared him and filled him with dread and antipathy.

On more than one occasion, dark winter was the worst, he would be in bed, invariably earlier than necessary, still awake waiting for sleep to descend, when he would hear the faint footsteps coming up the stairs. He would hold his breath in fear and also to ensure the noise of his laboured breathing didn't interrupt his aural acuity. If the steps continued on the flight that led to his room, he would close his eyes and feign sleep. The door would open quietly and someone would enter the room and stand by the entrance, barely audible. He knew who it was. It would never be anyone else. He lay there, tense with every sinew stiff and taut. Eventually, a soft, almost dolcet voice disturbed the hushed nocturnal silence which made it all the more sinister and threatening.

'So, Mr Danny, you think you are so clever, so special. Well, let me tell you, I'm as good as you could ever be. There is nothing you could teach me, nothing you know that I don't. You are not so clever, Mr Danny.'

He didn't say a word. He didn't want another row, he wanted to sleep, to be fresh for school. She wasn't totally convinced he was awake.

'Are you awake? I know you are awake..' she tempted, inviting a reply from the nine year old boy who lay still as a rock. He said nothing, not one word.

'You are here because I allow you to be here,' she continued. 'You aren't as clever as you think.'

He was lying next to Michelle, a different winter night, a different home. Their mother had just tucked them in and had pulled the curtains tight to prevent the morning light invade their dream filled reverie. She returned to the bed and bent over and kissed her daughter goodnight and then passing between the headboard and the wall, she glided her hand across her son's head and said goodnight, turned off the light and in the pitch black that consumed them, the door closed with a gentle thud.

'Mummy didn't kiss me goodnight!' he said sorrowfully. 'She kissed you goodnight! Why didn't she kiss me goodnight?'

'Don't be a cry baby,' said Michelle, 'she probably forgot. It doesn't matter.'

'But she kisses me goodnight *everynight*,' he said, tearfully. 'Why didn't she kiss me goodnight?'

He was genuinely saddened by her oversight. Such a small thing but to a six year old like the end of the world.

'Go to sleep,' said his sister, 'and tell her tomorrow and she will give you two kisses.' Her suggestion didn't diminish his sadness that his beloved mummy had forgotten to kiss him. However, not wanting to be called a cry baby again, he cried silently to himself wondering what he had done wrong.

He was almost scared out of his skin as the shadow leapt up in an explosion of presence from behind the headboard and assumed human form and was on him, kissing and cuddling and tickling him over and over. It was his mummy!! She had been hiding all along, listening to their conversation.

He chuckled as he tried to wriggle free from her tickling hands and he could hear Michelle who had turned over, startled too at first but then joining in with the laughter in vicarious pleasure at her mother's subterfuge. His mother gave him one last hug and said,

'I know you are awake, don't pretend to be asleep.' The voice stirred him from his drowsy, comforting memory. Grace was still in the room…

~~~~~~~~~~~~~~~~~~~~~

TWO HOSPITAL VISITS

The initial indications of his father's decline were so gradual that they could easily have gone unnoticed. Danny's grandmother had just died and he was now ten years old. His father had begun to complain of a sensation of wobbly legs and a feeling of lack of control over those lower limbs. No-one seemed overly concerned at the time and Gerrard Road life continued regardless. It was only when one day after his father had been on early turn and had awoken from an afternoon slumber that often followed those early starts, that the first suggestion of something more sinister became apparent.

His father had left the living room where he had been dozing and was at the base of the small set of stairs that led to the toilet. Danny happened to emerge from the kitchen just in time to see his father suddenly grab hold of those ramshackle bannisters and hold them tightly for support as both his legs began to dance independently of the rest of his body with a savage vibrancy. His feet never left the floor but the legs above swayed violently back and forth.

'Dad?? Are you ok, Dad?' said the startled boy.

'Yes, Danny,' replied his dad, trying to reassure but sounding a little startled himself. 'I'm fine. I just woke up but my legs are still sleepy,' he explained.

'Do you need a hand?' asked the boy.

'No, I'm fine, honest, go and play,' his father replied.

Danny turned as though to go into the living room and opened the door to give the impression that he was not unduly concerned nor paying attention, But as his father turned back to the toilet in front of him, the boy, hand on the door, kept his eyes fixed on his father's crouched shape.

His father began to move forward, slowly, tentatively, almost crab like as he moved each arm in unison with a lower limb, leg touching floor, hand gripping bannister. When he reached the space remaining between the last step and the toilet, he stretched out an arm to steady himself and then bridged the small gap with his leg in a high gait like motion and successfully entered the toilet.

This scene or scenes like it gradually became more common but sleepy legs could no longer be blamed. Even on just standing up when not in the thrall of post sleep trance, his legs would sometimes shake, not always but more often than previously. In several conversations that Danny overheard, a catalogue of possibilities were promulgated to explain the strange shaking leg syndrome. Maybe the emotional strain of tending a dying wife who had undergone a protracted illness was the cause, or perhaps the loss of his mother so soon after the first death was the breaking point. Then again, maybe it was a physical reaction to the mixers added to that brown liquid, a liquid which was assuming an increasing presence in the household.

From now on, no lemonade or fizzy additives to be blended with the whisky, just water. That was their solution. Danny didn't ever recall the brown stuff itself mooted as a possible candidate for blame.

Whatever the cause was, it soon became very clear that this affliction was not going to go away without some external assistance. Finally, his father went to the doctor.

Initial diagnoses proved inconclusive; various prescriptions were dispensed, physiotherapy recommended but no definitive classification of the illness if indeed it were an illness was proffered. None of the pills worked and nor did the physiotherapy and if anything, the shaking was becoming more pronounced. The only temporary antidote appeared to be a forceful application of his father's body weight on some fixed object to steady the trembling. A walking stick would provide the most practical method of ensuring a fixed object would always be available.

There hadn't been many games with his dad before but now, other than chess, there were none at all. This was becoming a little too familiar. Initially, his father still slept in the bedroom nearest to the front door and on those mornings when he wasn't working early, Danny who was normally already up and downstairs could hear the quiet, slow steps of his father negotiating the stairs to the kitchen. He used to time the descent but often lost interest or count as that trek seemed interminable. On those nights when his father was at home in the living room, the trek back up to his bedroom was equally laborious, not lessened in its difficulty by the whisky that had been consumed.

This state of affairs continued for a while, like a bouilder hurling down a crevice, hurtling to its destruction but temporarily finding respite on some jutting crag but only as long as the crag can resist the inexorable force above it until finally, overwhelmed, it breaks free, setting the boulder once more on its path to ruination.

There were some uncomfortable parallels that could be drawn here.

Danny was standing in the white, sanitised corridor of the hospital holding his daddy's hand, his sister on the other side holding the other hand.

'Your wife is in Farren Ward,' said the smiling white, sanitised nurse. 'Fourth bed on the right. Go straight in, she's been waiting for you.' They walked along the aisle into the large expanse that housed a row of beds on either side. Some of the areas were curtained and some were open to general view in which various incumbents lay or were sitting. Most of them had visitors, family members perhaps, friends, lovers, although some were alone, hopeful or resigned to their solitude. All the while, Danny was conscious of a funny smell, a clean type of smell, something that he would be tempted to drink, like fizzy ribena. He was wondering whether his mother's bed would be secluded by a mantle of fabric or whether it would be open to that general view.

As his father swept back a curtain just enough for the three of them to pass within, he had his answer. His mother was propped up, sitting against her raised pillows. The smile that radiated from her face as she saw them enter was a thing of unspeakable delight. Adorning her head was a tightly bound scarf so that none of her hair was visible. She opened her arms as wide as she was able and Danny and his sister rushed for an arm each which encircled them both as they rested in the bosom of their mother's embrace.

After innumerable kisses and hugs, they sat up, couched on the bed and their mother asked them questions of a trivial nature but which doubtless comforted her and them, as well as transporting her back to a temporary illusion of normality in circumstances which were all but normal.

Danny was trying to focus on his mother's words, providing acceptable responses when required and advising her that Cookie was well, watered and fed, but he couldn't help allowing his gaze to wander upwards when he thought she wasn't looking at him. That scarf was tight over her upper forehead and scalp, but when she raised her head, it moved slightly and allowed visual access to a small portion of the upper body part below the hairline. It was the reddened, slightly jagged line that ran round her forehead, near the top, which was distracting the boy's attention. He couldn't imagine what it was but as young as he was, he knew what a hospital signified. That knowledge, combined with his mummy being in a nightdress in the middle of the day with a scarf around her head hiding her hair and a red line running its circumference did not seem a good thing.

It was when the suggestion that a relatively new form of medical approach called acupuncture should be applied in an attempt to mitigate if not eradicate the presenting symptoms of his father's ailment, that the parallels seemed uncomfortably distinct. Once more Danny found himself by the bed of a hospitalised parent who had just undergone a clearly painful procedure. But this time there were certain disparities to the previous example. Five years difference was one. Danny was five years older. His perceptions were evolving, maturing.

He understood illness more at the tender age of ten than he had as the innocent bystander at five; he had seen people emasculated, disempowered by the onset of illness. He was becoming a veteran, more inured and less sensitive to the vagaries and uncertainty of life.

Furthermore, his mother had been vibrantly receptive, upright, delighted to see him and his sister, energetically welcoming them despite the awfulness of whatever had created that cylindrical scar probably only twenty-four hours previously which she wore like some badge of resistance. His father however, was everything his mother hadn't been; immobile, laid out, head slightly raised but body clearly avoiding any movement that was not necessary, and certainly, justifiably, more concerned about his own evident pain than the presence of his young children.

Danny had insiduosly manoeuvred the paper, the Sun, into his eyeline, devouring the script, trying to imagine the significance of the announcement that someone important called Nixon was going to visit somewhere remote called China. He was standing by the bed, next to his sister who was occupied in some pursuit of her own, although probably not engaged in the same fantasies as those that captivated her in that Hampstead lounge years before, when suddenly his father's arm stretched out and snatched the paper away when the three of them were alone.

'You came to see me,' he quietly shouted, clearly in discomfort. 'At least act as though you want to be here!'

But the fact was Danny really did not want to be there. It wasn't that Danny didn't care about his father or that he didn't love him. He deeply loved him.

But he just didn't want to be in a hospital again, or near another ill person, especially not his only surviving parent. Already in his young life he had seen enough. He was sorry his dad was unwell and he wished him well but surely, he thought, surely, this could not be all there was to life.

~~~~~~~~~~~~~~~~~~~~

THE SECOND FAILURE

Life at Gerrard Road continued; his father had returned to the fabric of everyday life following that ineffective sojourn in hospital. Both he and Grace plied their trades independent of each other whilst Michelle and Danny continued with their daily trek back and forth to the school that had come to replace their beloved Rosary. Within a relatively short passing of time, old friends were forgotten although in Danny's case not replaced. In that pre-secondary school era, free days were invariably passed in the confines of Gerrard Road with Martha as their overseer and monitor.

It was one such day when he was accompanying Martha to Chapel Market, a market still active today but much less patronised than the seventh decade of the twentieth century, when an idea came to him that quickly firmed up into concrete possibility. His father had started to show and teach him chess moves when he was four years old, and consequently, when they played as they had for the ensuing seven years, the boy's proficiency had developed sufficiently to demand a degree of respect and attention from the father who had to be increasingly wary lest the student vanquished the teacher. However, the board they used was of the basic genre, small wooden vassals and cheap plywood battle ground dimensions.

It was when they crossed over from Duncan Street to Upper Street that he saw it. The shop name he didn't observe but as they slowly walked past, he could clearly discern the price of the fabulously ornate pieces protruding and projecting their existence through the window of the small vendor's establishment.

An imperious couple decked in marble, king and queen, alongside them the officers of the church, the bishops sculpted like angry seraphims, then the horses strident and afoot, chained and buckled with imposing fortifications on either side, their bastions of support. Before the rank of nobility, the peasant line in anxious apprehension, awaiting the dictates of their fate. All of the protagonists seated upon the most magnificent board chiseled from some deep layered ore or mineral which was bedecked in smatterings of natural colour. Now *that* was a chess set! That would be a quite *marvellous* present for his ailing father and just in time for his fast approaching birthday! It may not make him better, he knew now that gifts were not the panacea that adverts would have one believe but it would certainly enliven his day with some element of joy and make him feel better.

Above the ranks of the opposing forces rose a flag that announced the price for the whole ensemble. £7.37. Immediately he saw the price, he knew his own financial coffers lacked the means to effect the full purchase. But this time, unlike the Ladybird books incident, he could enlist an entire array of personnel in his cause. He had met the other siblings of his father; Elsa came most Saturdays for lunch and whisky, Margaret was an infrequent guest and not well known to him and Bernard of course, could have bought it outright, that rich he seemed. Then there was Martha herself and maybe even Grace. But no matter if Grace refused to participate, after all, all those siblings had children, his cousins, they could be enlisted too. He even briefly considered asking the would be recipient of the gift to participate himself before rapidly abandoning that idea.

All in all, he would need about ten bob or so from each and every participant to actualise the purchase of that gift, that potential assuager of the discomfort of his father.

'Aunty Martha,' he began, used now to her responses and the need to navigate the conversation with adept dexterity.

'Yes?' she said, half heartedly as she contemplated the Sainsbury queues and the open stalls replete with green and pure fodder.

'Daddy isn't very well, is he?' he asked.

'Your daddy has got trembly legs, he will get better,' said the woman who had assured him he would see Dingdong again.

'But wouldn't it be nice if his family could help him get better?' he replied.

'His family *are* helping him get better,' said Martha.

'How?' he continued.

'Because we are are,' she said.

'How?' he persisted.

'Because we all support him,' she answered.

'I have an idea,' he said. She didn't acknowledge him. She was dismissing his views again. He had witnessed this before but this time he would bring inarguable logic to the table of commonsense and creative thinking.

'If we all buy him a present for Christmas or his birthday, then maybe he will see we all really want him to get better.' No answer. 'Aunty Martha,' he tugged at her sleeve but not with too much force. He didn't want to alienate her, just get her attention.

'What, Danny?'

'We could all buy him a present, me, you, Mitch, Aunty Elsa, Aunty Margaret, Uncle Bernard, Aunty Grace. It wouldn't cost much if we all paid a bit!' Aunty Martha realised this conversation had to be dealt with as it wasn't going to disperse by itself.

'Do you have any particular present in mind,' she enquired. He tried not to lead directly to his predetermined goal but he had not yet mastered the subtle technique of mental manipulation.

'Well, he plays chess, doesn't he?' he said, trying his best to delay direct vocalisation of his purpose, 'so maybe something to do with chess.'

'Possibly,' she answered, 'We can think about it another day.'

He realised that the conversation was getting away from him and that it would be difficult to re-visit the same topic on a disconnected occasion, not to mention the urgency that the imminent birthday injected into the plan.

He had to garner the support of one adult as his ally in his scheme for leverage with the other adults whose financial involvement would be critical, not to mention the need for a grown up to coalesce the various elements of the stratagem. Grace for the most obvious of reasons was not in the running for any approach. The most malleable adult and approachable of his aunts and uncles, (Winnie alas, featured no longer in that number) was Elsa. She was a gentle and kind woman whom he had come to know fairly well since his arrival at Gerard but there would be no opportunity to enlist her aid as her visits and consequent availability were limited and too intermittent. His aunt Margaret at this point he knew remotely and his uncle Bernard to whom he was very drawn, nonetheless seemed scary and unapproachable. Martha it had to be; she was the most practical conduit not least because he saw her most during the day. Furthermore, she had to some extent managed to shake free of that mantle of harridan façade that she had initially exhibited which is not to say he felt fully confident of her underlying motivation and sentiment about his and his sister's presence in Gerrard Road.

'Well, we could maybe look for something now, today, while we are shopping, couldn't we?' the boy added. 'After all, it's daddy's birthday in a few days time, so we don't have much time, do we?' he asked, using unknowingly an oft used psychological device in attempts to enlist collective support, namely, *'we'*. No answer. She wasn't deliberately disregarding his words so much as not really hearing them, more intent on whether to buy frozen ready made chips for Charlie's dinner or make them herself. Too many cigarettes and too many chips and not enough running on Hackney Marshes were ingredients of a dish that Charlie would one day grievously regret having ingested.

'What about that chess set back there?' he said abandoning any lingering attempt at disguising his purpose as desperation began to replace subtlety. 'It was lovely. Really lovely. And it only cost about seven pounds which isn't much if we get lots of people to pay a bit each.' She was still leading him by the hand and having to pull him more now as he tried to drop back and prevent the distance between them and the marbled ointment for his father growing too large. Still no answer. He stopped. 'Aunty Martha! Do you think it would be a good idea' – he extended his arm behind him in the direction of the shop they had recently passed- 'to buy that chess set for Daddy?' Martha had to stop and give Danny some attention now.

'What are you talking about?' she said crisp and curtly.

'I think it would be a really good idea if everyone paid some money and all bought that chess set back there for daddy's birthday,' he explained again patiently, not at all irritated that she seemed to be hearing this suggestion for the first time. The successful outcome was much more important than any obstacles in its realisation. 'Come and have a quick look, you will love it!' he said, turning and now pulling her in the other direction. He managed to get her back to the window where the chess set sat imperiously in the centre.

'Look!' said the boy, quickly digesting the whole image with his own eyes not sure how long he would have before the image would be but a memory.

He briefly glanced up to see if Martha was as fixated on the set as was he, to get some idea of her thoughts. He needed something else, a clincher.

He began to mouth the words but then looked at the middle aged woman, with little education and no interest in much besides shopping and cooking and tending her family and considered what he was about to say. It sounded lame and he held out little hope for success but that was all he could think of, that was all that was left, make the chess set seem useful to her too.

'And maybe you would like to learn to play chess, Aunty Martha. Me and daddy could teach you too on that beautiful board...' The words didn't even register, so alien a concept that it would have been to that adult.

'Come on, Danny, we have to go.' They moved back in the direction whence they had come.

'Well, Aunty Martha, shall we ask them all to buy it for Daddy?' there was that *we* again. Martha stopped, this time of her own accord and looked at him.

'Danny,' she began, 'are you really thinking about it as a present for your father or is it really a present for you?' He looked at her, shocked, genuinely, profoundly, deeply shocked, wounded that this thought had even entered her mind as it had certainly never entered his own!

He was so taken aback, so stunned that this had even been a possible interpretation that words failed briefly to materialise and she must have mistaken his lack of response for an admission of guilt as she turned and walked off with steeled foot, prepared to tolerate no further resistance; there *was* no more resistance as her response and his amazement to it had deflated his zealous enthusiasm, totally blindsided him.

All he could do was think over and over how she could even have thought that! She probably never heard him as he mumbled out loud to no one in particular. 'It wasn't for me, it wasn't, it was for my daddy.'

~~~~~~~~~~~~~~~~~~~~~~

THE CHEESE ROLL

By the time the boy had reached the latter stages of his fourteenth year, a walking stick had become an integral and permanent companion in his father's life. It had become familiar and developed a semblance of humanity that was absurd given its wooden animation. But it was part of his father and was as meaningful and useful as a surgical prosthetic. Danny was now at secondary school, his sister too. Both brother and sister possessed good minds; in fact, none of their cousins on their father's side -they had at this point lost total contact with their mother's smaller contingent- lacked mental ability. Danny was a fast thinker, avaricious reader of books; he had unintentionally begun the process of substituting emotional development for cerebral evolution years before, not too long after his mother's death, and would always be more at home with clinical logic than emotional expression.

By now he could aid his father in the completion of the Telegraph cryptic, he could beat him at chess with ease, he could understand the construction of Latin and Ancient Greek with seamless fluidity as these were languages predicated on pure logic and systemic rules that were easy to follow and allowed no emotional interpretation.

To ask a bookseller in Camden Passage for a copy of War and Peace at ten years old would be pretentious if the book were never read, but it was read. And it was read with passion, the names to remain forever embedded in the imagination, gallant Russian Pierres, noble Natashas, audacious Andres.

The love of Russia, the love of foreign climes, it all began in those Tolstoy passages. There was no pretension, only refuge from emotional horror that infested and underpinned his life. Books and reading. Escapism. Better than real life.

He had passed his 11 plus and the preferred choice of grammar school was the Cardinal Vaughan in Holland Park, educational edifice for his cousins, Martin and Philip. Martin had already left school when Danny began his first year but Phil was still there albeit five years in front of him. He had no say in the choice naturally, but it was considered prudent once more by the council of elders, presumably Grace, Martha and his father that this would be the ideal option since he could commute with his older cousin until he was old enough to commute alone. Michelle had passed the 11 plus too, and she had started her own grammar school education almost two years before he did. She was once more compelled to employ the good offices of the London Underground as would Danny. Her trip was short. Angel to Euston. Northern line. Three stops in total. She had no precedent though, no older female cousin to act as her introducing agent. Perhaps that was why the elders had decided on a more accessible location. He wondered who had taken her there in her early induction into secondary school, almost certainly Martha he supposed.

The first day Danny boarded the northern line en route to his own secondary school, he couldn't help recall the irony of his Aunt Martha's comment the day she had sought to use the dirty and smelly tube as an excuse, a reason to change school.

'You will like this school more, it is nearer, we can walk, so we wont have to use those smelly old trains again.' Well, he couldn't walk to Holland Park, that was for sure.

To an 11 year old it was miles away. And it actually was and remains miles away. There were two routes that were the most effective. The first and quickest was the northern line from the Angel to Kings Cross or Euston, then change onto the Victoria line which stopped at Warren Street and then Oxford Circus where another change was required onto the Central line calling at Bond Street, Marble Arch, Lancaster Gate, Queensway, Holland Park. That was the quick route...

The fallback route was still from the Angel but on the other side of the platform, Old Street, Moorgate and Bank, then change onto the Central line and call at St Paul's, Chancery Lane, Holborn, Tottenham Court Road, then Oxford Circus where this route merges with the first for its onward journey. Less changes with this route but more stops and all in all up to ten minutes longer.

Ten minutes may seem irrelevant in itself but as all inveterate commuters know, ten minutes comes to adopt significant meaning in a trip that goes on day after day, week after week, year after year; the meaning of those minutes that is carved from those accumulated hours is the balance between temporal precision and chaotic annihilation of the finest and intricate planning that hung on a knife edge.

Danny learnt from Phil as Phil had learnt from his brother Martin, and those boys lived on seconds, timed to perfection, knowledge honed by experience, the walk from the house to the station, the approximated wait for the first train, mentally allowing for delays, the walk from one changing post to the next, sprint speed if necessary, more time for pedestrian pace if each stage of the process was on schedule, the margin for error calculated like the finest technological machinery, nothing left to chance, every step considered.

Knowing how long they could wait, almost to the second, before they had to move to their fallback position and adopt the alternative route. Normal arrival 08.02-08.05 at the Angel. It was the time outside the train that was in their control, when they could decide to run or walk according to the rapidly unfolding events of those elements beyond their control, such as punctuality of those burrowing cylinders or hold ups in the tunnels between stasis. 08.09, 08.11 the latest they could take the Bank Route if no Kings Cross/Euston train was forthcoming.

All this just to avoid being late for a school which was miles away and yet in seven years, Danny was late for school twice. Twice. Just twice. Had that commuting been poetry, it would be nothing less than lyrical genius.

However, when the malevolent and deliberate hand of man sought to sabotage the proceedings, all the preparation in the world would make little difference. In this case man's hand belonged to a woman. The hand of Grace. Danny didn't have school dinners. He didn't know why, it just always was. He would take a roll to school in his packed lunch. A crusty and shapeless thing, not purchased from a bakers but from the little shop at the bottom of Gerrard Road that seemed to sell everything other than food except for a handful of white rolls that appeared as soon as it opened each day and were purchased almost as quickly.

Every morning he would run down to that shop, twenty seconds to get there, ten seconds to purchase said item, twenty seconds to run back, one minute for Grace to butter the roll and shove some cheese in its interior.

Done. It was always a rush. The shop rarely opened before 8am. The clock was ticking, the window of temporal accuracy was narrow. He had to be at the Angel by 08.05 to guarantee punctuality, the latest, the very latest 6 minutes later and it took at least two minutes to get there no matter how fast he ran. He didn't want to be late, that would result in being in trouble and detention but equally he didn't want to go without his lunch. It had happened once before and all day without food was an ordeal that was not happily repeated.

The cheese roll incident took place some considerable time after his cousin was no longer his travelling companion. Phil had finished his education and had set off to forge a career path, a path along which he was destined to advance far. Danny was on his own but he was used to it by now. The first time that there had been no Phil however, had been a very different matter. Danny was in his first year and had travelled for the initial term in the company of his sapient cousin. That day in the kitchen when he heard Martha descending the stairs -he was well conversant with which steps belonged to which person- one early morning when he was ready awaiting his cousin's rapid descent, he knew something was not as it was normally.

'Philip's not well,' she began. 'He wont be going to school today.' Danny's dad was in the room, as was Grace.

'Fair enough,' said the father. 'Dan will have to stay home today too then, he can't go by himself.' Just what Danny was thinking, but equally aware that he wasn't really unwell and this wasn't like baby school, a day off would mean a lot of catching up and also questions about his lack of attendance.

'Yes he can!' said Martha. 'He knows the way and he is a big enough boy to go alone, aren't you, Danny?' Martha had a lot of influence at that time. Perhaps his father and Grace deferred to her greater experience in raising children, perhaps she was more used to decision making for greater numbers of people, dictatorial even.

Danny was thinking rapidly as he looked at her, rehearsing, memorising the route in his own mind. It was relatively straightforward he thought. And he would rather risk that then have to worry all day what the reaction of his form master would be tomorrow if he was absent. Danny tended to worry about a lot of things.

'Yes,' he said, even before the full trip had been played out in his own mind. 'I can go by myself.' It was settled. Danny kissed his father goodbye and set out. The Angel to King's Cross was fine, he had elected King's Cross rather than Euston because it was the first stop after the Angel. However, this was an error. King's Cross provided the area of difficulty. It was a much bigger station with many more connections. He got lost. Suddenly, alone, those tunnels brimming with commuters, all resembled each other. Where was the Victoria line? He wasn't used to reading the signs, to date he had had no need since his cousin knew the path by rote and he simply followed, gradually becoming equally au fait with the route but clearly he hadn't quite yet mastered it yet.

He walked back and forth, following this crowd then that, trying to spot some familiar landmark but was aware he was becoming a little tearful with this inability to locate his bearings and the prospect of being late appearing on the horizon.

He was 11, surely he should be able to negotiate this simple task. It seemed like hours he was coursing these halls of white brick, he was sure he would be late, when somehow suddenly, he was on the right platform. He had reached the Victoria line. He leant back against the curvature of the wall of the platform and felt a surge of relief. He had found his way and he wouldn't be late.

The day of the cheese roll, two years later, wasn't about lack of directional ability; it was about malign sabotage. Danny was in the kitchen and the hour was nearing 07.54. There was little difference at this point to most other days. There was only he and Grace in the kitchen and as usual, he was waiting for her to dispense 5 pence so he could race down the road. There was no more Philip companionship. 07.56.

'Can I have the money please, Grace?' he asked timidly, ever wary of her volatile and potentially cruel temperament.

'Yes, in a minute,' she said standing by the fridge next to the kitchen door. He didn't like to keep asking but he was conscious of time constraints and he knew that she too was conscious of them. 07.58.

'Aunty Grace,' he hated having to be obsequious to this loathsome woman, but he had to feign courtesy, to simulate servitude, all he wanted was five pence and a bit of cheese inside the roll that the five pence would buy, 'I will be late if I don't leave for the roll now and they may all get sold.'

'I said in a minute,' she answered, not looking at him. Yes he thought, you said in a minute five minutes ago. She was being purposely difficult.

Nothing, *nothing* was preventing her from giving him that five pence at that very moment other than lack of volition and spite.

He was standing behind her, silently hopping from foot to foot. She *knew* how much good time keeping meant to him. How he went to bed early so that he would always be up punctually, even if often he couldn't sleep for hours. She knew too, how his school frowned upon tardiness and his natural leaning was to stay off the radar as much as he could. She also knew this. And it was this knowledge that told him she was being wilfully intransigent since giving him the five pence now or five pence later would have no deleterious impact on her at all whereas the delay for him could have catastrophic ramifications. Pleaseeee, he thought, please just open your purse and give me the money. 08.03.

'Aunty Grace, look at the time. Please, please can you let me have five pence and I'll run down for the roll? I am going to be late for school if I don't go soon.'

'I said in a minute! Just wait!'

The minutes ticked by, he checked his bag, he looked at his watch, he looked for signs she was readying her purse. It was like the door of a bank vault opening, the inertia needing to build as it began its laboured movement. She turned to her bag, and dug around inside seeking her purse. 08.06. He was really agitated now, it couldn't be right that a child should undergo this much stress before the day was fully in motion. 08.08. He was by her shoulder, on tiptoes, seeking the money with his eyes, willing its appearance. There it was!

'There, take that, and get your roll.'

'Thank you,' he said as he was off in full flow, up those four steps, then the main flight, at the front door, latch on without interrupting his sprint to the shop. He was there in a flash, no queue, small mercies, and there were a few rolls left, one of which he grabbed.

'Hello, young man, you are a little late,' voiced the Polish accent. 'Let me get you a bag for that.'

'No time Mr Tomawicz,' he said. 'No need for the bag' he continued breathlessly, 'have to go, thanks,' as he handed over the money. He was running again, up the street, beads of sweat, the product of intense activity and anxiety, daubing his forehead and arms, back into Gerrard and down the stairs.

'There, Aunty Grace, please, *please* hurry! Please!' he was pleading. He grabbed his bag whilst keeping one eye on her progress. He was late, very late, these minutes meant everything and she was still buttering the roll. 'Don't worry about both sides,' he said 'and no need for a bag, I will put it in my case.' She was cutting the cheese, it was 08.10. Finally. He snatched it. Thanks. And he was off again.

Up the stairs, out the door, sprinting up the road, turning left into Colebrook Row, along the hundred metre length of the park where he had outrun his father, onwards to the end of the street, then right into Pentonville Road and the entrance to the station. As he ran into the entrance hall he scanned the lift status, nothing there, he couldn't linger, didn't hesitate, decision made, down the emergency stairs, all 224 of them, two at a time where he could, rapid one by ones where he couldn't.

He could hear a train, he knew the sounds, back of his hand, it was a north bound train, the type of noise betrayed the route, it was the fast route, via Kings Cross, he could make up time, he ran harder, breathing laboured, young lungs heaving, he dodged commuters, he skimmed the walls, experience was playing its role, he arrived at the top of the stairs to the platform as the train pulled in, down two at a time, doors opening, in he went. 08.12. No sitting, against the door, ready to leap out, move to the next staging post, brief respite, catch his breath, King's Cross, he would go on to Euston, quicker. Doors opened, off he went, up the stairs, two at a time, running though the passage, ears intent on noises, listening for approaching Vicoria line, there it was, pulling in, the noise propelled him, faster, down the last escalator, doors closing, on board he leapt, Oxford Circus next, last stage. 08.24. He had 16 minutes left.

No matter what happened now, he was going to have to sprint from Holland Park tube all the way down Holland Pak Avenue to school. He was sodden with sweat. He ran from the Victoria line at Oxford Circus to the Central and once more small mercies assisted his cause, a train was pulling into the station. All the way from the Circus to the Park he stood by the door, scouring the carriage for similar uniforms but finding none, confirmation of tardiness, anxious, checking his watch, willing the train to go faster, finally arriving and not even considering the lift as he sprinted up the 93 emergency stairs, then out of the station and away, pushing as hard as he could, faster , faster, a few stragglers in the same uniform as his own. He could barely breathe but Addison Road was in sight. He crossed the main road with indifferent abandon and passed the old part of the school and then into the main entrance to his own area.

Assembly bell had sounded but he was at the tail end of the throng going in. He was last but he wasn't late. And he had beaten Phil's record time! What a start to the school day, all over a rotten old cheese roll…

~~~~~~~~~~~~~~~~~~~~~~~

THE CHESS GAME

Danny was sitting on a stool in the living room playing chess with his father who was sitting opposite under the window that gave the impression of amputated legs. From this position however, the periodic passers by were vertically upright and fully visible. He was well on his way to fifteen now and all those hormones that are crucial for the preservation of humanity were in full flow inside his being. He was developing a teenage arrogance, not as pronounced as his peers as he was always wary of self-promotion. With his father however, he could exhibit more confidently some of the swagger that he would not feel comfortable exhibiting anywhere else. He had also begun to notice girls in a different way and those things that had been viewed once upon a time with such innocent wonder were now seen from a different perspective. Even the window above him which was once a source of wonder from the viewpoint of truncated souls was now more a source for peering up the skirts of any wearer of such who happened by.

First impressions could lead to the conclusion that Danny was something of a drip; not from the way he looked, although his dress sense was hardly high fashion, but from his habits. He was a fine chess player, an avid reader and a first rate student of Latin and Ancient Greek language and literature. He was a train spotter too, who could differentiate between a Brush 2 and a Brush 4 (it was all about the windows) and the fiery shape of a Deltic. In his defence however, his train spotting habit had come into existence as a cover for a less innocuous pastime. These type of pursuits could easily be misconstrued and lead to a belief of geeky persona.

The truth as often is the case was very different from the assumption; the reading and the study were escape outlets from a world which had to date proved too cruel to bear. Literature was a more gentle and sanitised bedfellow than reality. Being absorbed in a book was a most wonderful inroad into a theatre of fiction and imagined characters who had their paths mapped out for them and where no real emotional damage was wrought nor irreparable pain caused. It was possible to engage with those characters and even if the fate of those literary mannequins was not always the most savoury of endings, at least the content could be subsumed for what it was, fiction.

Chess was simply a game that for some reason both his father and his uncle Bernard played and a natural progression was for the boy to be shown how to play too. His father was not very good, but compared to Bernard, he was practically Bobby Fischer. His uncle was dreadful, quite dreadful. The pair of them didn't even know the full rules and for years Danny had thought that the castling manoeuvre was quite different from what the rules actually stated. It was the mighty Pole, his uncle Roman, Elsa's husband who corrected him. In that era, the cold war was fully in swing and chess was often used as a bloodless battle between the Soviet Union and the United State as some representation of superiority. The world championships in this era were dominated by those two superpowers.

The matches between Spassky the Russian and Fischer the maniacal American genius in the 1972 Reykjavik World Championship were legendary. Their progress could be charted in the Evening Standard in the games section which also featured a daily puzzle, mate in two's, mate in three's and so on, compiled by the great Leonard Barden.

So of course, the first time Daniel played his Polish uncle, he was already disadvantaged and intimidated by the psychological knowledge that this man was an Eastern European whose country formed part of the Soviet prowess that was their chess powerhouse. He lost. He lost a lot. It didn't take too long though, until Danny realised the truth about that lovely man. That Polish powerhouse, that gargantuan Soviet export of chess domination, that formidable bastion of a board game that represented a struggle of global proportions, was actually rubbish. He wasn't much better than the other males in his family, although at least he knew the rules. It wasn't long before Danny was destroying him too.

There were other facets to Danny's character that could equally indicate a certain social ineptitude, an awkwardness in arenas with which he wasn't overly familiar. Ever since his mother's death and his transfer into that stunted and derelict emotional wasteland, his emotional and social development was somewhat arrested. Other than the early days when he strove to protect his sister and they hugged each other, and again when he returned from his Spanish trip, there was little affection in that house. He didn't even hug his sister nor her him the day she brought him more fateful news a few years later. He NEVER hugged Grace, he could barely even bring himself to kiss her if he was ever compelled to do so and he certainly would NEVER have volunteered her a kiss; his father too, few hugs, few kisses, although there would be one significant kiss in the not too distant future. And then there was the lack of social communion, the active *discouragement* to have friends anywhere near their place of residence. Not one friend from any school ever saw the inside of his home. Although on reflection in later life, he would come to think that that may have been a good thing given its grotesque demeanour.

Throughout his school career, he went to the home of one fellow pupil (which incidentally had a bath, a shower, no lice and a bedroom for his friend who was permitted to install his books and anything else that belonged to him). Consequently, social niceties, elegant public comport, these were features simply lacking to him. Michelle didn't have the same inadequacy or at least didn't appear to possess it. Again, perhaps it was the age difference, or maybe just a more robust soul or maybe an amalgamation of both. He could remember a number of times when she was to be found in the kitchen with a new friend she had acquired, invariably short lived, neither she nor Danny were particularly adept at retaining long term friendships or relationships and even when they did, they would do their utmost to sabotage them.

She also went out more than he did; one day when he was about thirteen, she decided to invite him along. Maybe she felt sorry for his isolation, maybe she was just being sisterly, their bonds hadn't yet been entirely undone. It was a Saturday. About ten in the morning.

'I'm going to see Francesca,' she said to him. 'She's got a brother, a bit younger than you. Marco. You can come too if you like.'

'Who's Francesca?'

'She's a friend of mine.'

'Where do they live? What school does her brother go to?' he asked trying to prepare a framework in which he could feel comfortable.

He wanted to go; it was an adventure, something to do.

'Ok. I'll come,' he said decisively.

They made their way to the house wherein resided Francesca and her brother Marco, sister leading the way. They walked; it didn't take too long. Michelle seemed totally free of nerves or concern. He, on the other hand, was apprehensive and timid. They arrived at the block which Michelle told him contained their dwelling, a flat, and walked up steps to the second floor. There were about five floors and each level had a small, stout and stocky wall running its entire length acting as a barrier against the outside world and a defence system against the drop to the pavement below. There were loads of doors on each floor, all remarkably similar to each other and there was a good deal of concrete in evidence.

'This is the one,' said Michelle as she raised the door knocker and let it drop back to its starting position. Danny straightened his clothes and pushed back his hair with a sweep of his hand. As he saw a shape approach the door through the frosted upper portion of the glass that was embedded in the frame, he pushed his hair back again, trying to flatten it with the flat of his hand. The door opened and there was a small, dark haired, foreign looking woman who was on the portly side of thin but whose smile radiated warmth and welcome.

'Hello, hello!' she cried enthusiastically, in an accent that reminded him of the Spanish he had heard abroad. 'You must be Michelle and this is...'

'That's Danny,' said his sister, 'my younger brother.'

'Oh hello, Danny! Enter, enter, you are both welcome...' she added, extending her hand whilst stepping back to allow greater aperture for the door. Danny smiled back and followed her sister into the flat. The front door entered directly into the lounge, where the central piece was an old and worn brown three seat settee, an isle in the middle of the expanse of the home.

However, as he looked more closely, he saw that this room was cluttered like his own home, full of old things, used but homely. That was where the similarity stopped though. There was no dirt, no immediate indications of dereliction, just a place where feeling at home was the thematic thread that permeated the space. The stout, smiling woman made the introductions, Michelle needed none with Francesca and greeted Marco, paying lip service to basic courtesty before moving to the end of the lounge with her friend and leaving Danny to pay more regard to the young man standing at his shoulder height. Michelle was right, he was younger but not only slightly! He was at least three years or so junior, bronzed skin, aquiline features with straight cropped hair, not too dissimilar to Sandro, and clearly very interested in his older male guest.

The woman gestured to the settee and Danny sat, in the middle, while his new compatriot ran out of the lounge and into what was presumably his bedroom. He returned rapidly clutching a board game but not offering it, just seeing how its presence in his arms would be received. Danny said nothing. He didn't know who was shier. Michelle was busily engaged in fervent chatter with Francesca every now and then casting a watchful eye in Danny's direction making sure he was alright.

The portly woman had left the living room and had entered the small kitchen clearly visible through the *tendina* that framed the entrance thereto. The young Marco stood by the arm of the settee, waiting for some guidance from the older boy. Danny didn't know what to say.

Michelle was glancing over more, involved in her own dealings with her friend but clearly distracted until her brother had settled in. Danny was sitting upright as he clasped his right shin with both hands and began rocking back and forth displaying a pose of relaxed confidence, a measured and fabricated smile enhancing the posture. What was not visible however, was his thought process that was desperately seeking some words, *any* words, that when placed together might create a cogent sentence and break the ice.

He was desperately thinking of a comment or question that would animate the proceedings but nothing came to mind. He struggled even at that time with meaningless small talk. However, he was conscious of the need to say something. The little boy by him was hunched over the arm of the settee, observing some arbitrary pattern on the cover or some other diverting aspect of life. He had to say something, anything.

'So,' he said, ' do they do Latin at your school?'

What was that he had just said?? Latin?? *Do they do Latin at your school?* What?? Had he really said that? As soon as the words had left his lips, Danny wished he knew how to beat his own face in with his fists. Really?? Do they do Latin? Was that the best he had to offer? Was there nothing else he could have come up with? The polite young man shook his head and Danny issued a knowing, 'Ahh! I see.'

But all he really saw was the horror of the question he had offered. He truly was a drip.

A similar lack of social grace revealed itself in his late teens when he had applied and been accepted for a job at a company search business which was commissioned by solicitors and accountants to execute various inquiries on corporations and individuals for the purposes of uncovering extant liability in potential purchases or takeovers.

It was a dull and dreary job, running into company house in Old Street, collecting fiches and then analysing the fiches for debentures, cautions or charges and the like. The job was temporary however and it was close to the Angel, one stop on the northern line but he always walked or jogged. There were a number of young, itinerant people who were using the post as a stepping stone or interim position and the owners didn't mind, they got bright people who learned quickly and so the turnover was easily managed.

He became friends with Maggie. She had a minor squint in one eye and thick, short bushy blonde hair. She was his age and intelligent as well as being quite arty and they used to lunch together on the bench in the centre of Old Street roundabout which lacked the floral and fauna that bedecks its current compass.

The problem was the food; he loved his cherry pie. But so did she. A little too much. Initially, they would purchase their respective lunches from the proximal food halls, a cheese roll with some seductive sauce or a salmon sandwich with a twist of lemon and then some dessert to complement the wheat based main course.

His sweet choice was always the cherry pie from the same location. He loved it. The plan from early on was that they would taste each other's food. It was *her* plan however; he wasn't overly enamoured by the concept but his testosterone levels manufactured whatever approach it felt most effective to implement the biological imperative and for a while he went along with it. As he observed her teeth incising his sandwich and depositing a residual slither of saliva, he squirmed but tolerated it..

The day she took a bigger chunk of his cherry pie than was appropriate was the breaking point. He didn't express his disgust in words to her, he actually said nothing. He just picked up his remaining pie, got up and without saying a word to her, walked back to the office and never spoke to her again. Not a word. He just refused to speak to her, primal directives or not. She had no idea what she had done. She tried to initiate a dialogue but he was having none of it. He didn't know how.

The table in between Danny and his father was not only occupied by the chess board. It was also occupied by a glass of whisky, an ashtray filled with innumerable tipless butts, a lighter, a hooked handle of the permanent feature that was the walking stick and Danny's burgeoning, arrogant swagger. He could see his father was a little drunk, the eyes gave it away not to mention his own increasing familiarity with the effect of the brown liquid. In the background, music emanated from a small Philips tape recorder. His cousin Philip had a fabulous stereo system, Danny had seen it, graphic equaliser, SEA apparently, big dual speakers, and vinyl playability. The Philips tape recorder was a banquet to a pauper.

'Does this tape player have the ability to repeat the same song automatically?' asked his dad.

'No, Dad, it isn't 4-track. But I can rewind it if you like.'

'Yes, please do that.'

'Ok.' Danny got up, smiling inwardley at his technological superiority and strutted over to the small tape machine. Man of La Mancha, To Dream The Impossible Dream, Don Quixote and tilting at windmills was the refrain.

Walking for his father, even the most modest distance, was becoming more and more belaboured. A natural act taken for granted now reduced to an entire process of positioning stick in correct spot, attempting to rise, and then manoeuvring into place before beginning the walking phase itself. It wouldn't be long before a wheelchair replaced the stick.

The opening of the chess match was past and they were well into the middle game and Danny was paying scant regard as he knew he would win regardless of his father's responsive moves. He was miles away, a little bored, needing to test his developing macho power.

'Why do you like this music so much anyway,' he said, looking for a verbal contest, confident he could rebut his father's retorts with witty and clever parries. His father was crouched over the board, a man whose spirit was lost and featureless, sipping his whisky and pulling on his cigarette.

'Because I dreamt the impossible dream once,' he said in slurred tones.

'Yeah, yeah' said his scornful, swaggering son, dismissive of the man before him. 'Drunken talk again.'

'Ok Danny,' said his father, sympathetically, 'I hope you never have to dream an impossible dream.'

'As if you have ever had to do so other than with that stuff,' he said scathingly, accusingly, sneeringly, pointing at the whisky.

'But I did,' said his father.

'Sure you did,' said his son, dismissive and cynical. Silence other than the music. Danny couldn't leave it, baiting, provoking his loving father.

'What impossible dream did *you* ever have?' he asked, looking at his father with unmasked disgust. His father raised himself up from his hunched position and looked tearfully at his son.

'I dreamt of keeping your mother alive.'

There was no delay, no hesitation, no time for comeback. Danny immediately lowered his head as the silent tears welled up, trying to pretend his father's comment had gone unnoticed but it was like a knife to his heart, all the swagger, all the false arrogance dissolved at once. He hadn't seen that coming. Not for a moment. He may have won the game but it was he who had been checkmated.

~~~~~~~~~~~~~~~~~~~~~

COUSIN PHIL

By the time Danny was in his final year at St John's, it was clear that he was one of the two brightest pupils in the year. The other was an extremely clever, bespectacled, frizzy haired girl and all the remaining class members knew these two were the most valuable members for the teams of the intermittent quiz sessions. Years later, Danny would find that young girl who had matured into an adult woman on Friends Reunited and she would admit to him that secretly she knew he had the edge. That they were both head and shoulders above the rest was the only definitive fact. She passed the 11-plus as did he, indeed, as did a number of others and they all went their separate paths to their respective academic destinies.

The first day he arrived at Cardinal Vaughan, he was overwhelmed by the newness and magnitude of the whole event. He had travelled with Philip as he would for the few years his cousin had remaining on his academic journey. This was big boys' school and a whole new ethos was immediately evident. Cardinal Vaughan did and still does, comprise two buildings, one for the first to third years, and the other, more modern building for the rest, including the sixth formers. The younger boys' building was austere and red bricked and resembled with striking similarity Colditz, a book Danny had recently been reading, not least the small, triangular shaped playground that was overlooked by three, high walls resembling a prison compound.

Two things were immediately apparent; discipline and cleanliness. It was foreboding. It was scary. The frivolous, relaxed atmosphere of junior school was replaced by a more business like approach to academic excellence. These seminal moments like the first day at school in a child's life have levels of stress that are perhaps accorded less attention than they deserve but maybe the adapting nature of humanity and its inbuilt ability for change has already catered for such stressful episodes. At that moment, the only thing that Danny was looking forward to was being re-united with his cousin for the trip home.

Philip was a complicated soul. Danny didn't really know him and they could never really be described as friends in that Gerrard Road period. They would become much better friends in later life but for the moment Danny and his dad and sister were latecomers to the constitution of Gerrard, and Philip would have viewed them more as intruders than companions.

Philip himself was something of an outsider, always second fiddle to his older brother who shined academically and lit up the eye of his mother Martha. It wasn't that Martin courted favouritism so much as Martha dispensed it in his direction. Of course, she loved both her sons but there seemed to be a clear distinction between the level of attention she allocated to each. Martin was in the top stream of his school year, Philip the lowest. This is not to suggest nor imply that Philip wasn't bright; it was after all, a grammar school of the 70's and 80's when even the lower streams were still populated by clever minds. It was more that subconsciously, the pecking order had been established and fulfilled in one of those self-fulfilling precepts.

Danny didn't really have much cause or opportunity to know Martin who was much older and who had left the Vaughan long before Danny set out on his scholarly path. Philip however, was his travelling companion back and forth to that distant place of learning and naturally, constringent circumstance led to greater acquaintance between the two.

That notwithstanding, Philip was a withdrawn soul, suffering the full suffocation of his mother's domineering presence. He too, rarely had friends call. There was one, well favoured by his mother and who was allowed access but after he had departed, Phil stayed on to complete his A-levels and the replacement friend was less well received even though to Danny's young mind, the replacement seemed affable and pleasant. Philip was contaged by the Gerrard Road ethos of isolation which was not most ideal preparation for the development of social skills.

But Philip wasn't an entirely lame and emasculated social eunuch. Not too long after a very young Michelle and Danny had begun their smoking careers on a diet of stolen Number 6 or hijacked Embassy filters, it was Philip who had introduced them to the overpowering grandeur and length of Rothmans elite which dwarfed their existing brands. He appeared to them like some savant and executor of all things rebellious and non conformist. Given the lack of opportunity for those young people to smoke without risk of discovery, it was, once again, Philip who had cleverly engineered a train spotting hobby to which Danny was invited, along with the new friend who had replaced the beloved previous inhabitant of the role, so that they could puff away to their heart's content under the pretext of filling a small book with numbers of transient and fleeting trains at the end of a Waterloo platform. Electrical multiple units predominantly.

Danny naturally had more contact with Phil than did his sister, what with the daily trip to Holland Park and the occasional excursions to Hackney Marshes in which Michelle took part only once. It was Philip's idea to inject some interest into the mundane, daily commute by developing the idea of the BB's, the British Boys; those cousins would pretend on the walk home from the Angel station to the house, to be Olympic entrants, top drawer walkers, going for gold, and all those pedestrians in front of them would be unknowing participants in the contest, as the boys would seek to pass everyone ahead on the way to top podium position. They even came up with names to give their fictional heroes identity. Philip decided on *Fred Smith* and Danny introduced *Erebus* remembering how he had moulded some amorphous structure out of plaster of Paris at St John's and labelled it Erebus since it looked a little bit volcanic. Fred Smith and Erebus battled it out for two years, against each other and the rest of the world. It was a great game.

There was a fundamental difference between him and his cousin though. Philip had a caring mother greeting his daily homecoming, and more often than not with a cooked meal all prepared. For some reason, Martha would send him downstairs when they returned from school to join Michelle and Danny in the kitchen and then convey his dinner from upstairs which he would eat whilst Danny and his sister occupied themselves in homework or some other activity.

Michelle and Danny didn't eat their dinner then; they had to await Grace's return at about 6pm most nights and even then, she would not normally start cooking for at least an hour, depending on her mood, her energy levels, amount of brown stuff ingested and whether an argument broke out.

That wasn't so bad; Danny got used to it. Sometimes he even felt sorry for Phil having a dinner thrust before him as soon as he had returned from the gladiatorial arena of the juvenile institution called school. Philip himself was clearly reluctant to eat immediately on his return home. He didn't do himself any favours by his almost daily post school purchase of a bag of chips and fizzy drink which he would savour and devour on the Central line leg of the trip home, filling himself up knowing full well dinner would be waiting. Every afternoon, Martha opened the door to them, asking Philip threateningly if he had eaten chips as it would prevent him eating his dinner and Philip would unwaveringly deny it. But Phil could be surprisingly creative.

One day, in Danny's first year, still young and thinking in linear fashion, he and his cousin arrived home as normal, Philip as usual having gorged himself on his chips and fanta, and went downstairs where Michelle was already ensconced. As normal, Martha who had let them in, went upstairs leaving the three of them to their own devices whilst she put the finishing touches to her younger son's supper before bringing it down. They were all sitting at the table, that blue and white rickety thing, Philip in the centre, his knife and fork laid out before him, Michelle and Danny at either end. Philip was quiet, tapping the table with his fingers, clearly rapt in thought. Danny was in innocent, playful mode.

'What shall we play, Philly?' he asked. Michelle was uninterested, busying herself in her own enterprises. 'Chess?', he persisted. No answer. Phil had his head turned to the right and seemed intent on a point in virtuality.

'Oh go on, Phil! I'm bored! Let's play something. Please!'

Danny quite enjoyed these moments with his big cousin, they injected some variety into the structured, repetitive days of his existence.

'How about I-spy then?' Dan knew he didn't have much time to play as Martha would soon arrive with Phil's repast and following the ingestion thereof, Phil would be off upstairs for the rest of the day. After some delay, Philip spoke up.

'Ok,' he said, 'I've a game for us. A pretend game.'

'Great!' said Danny enthusiastically. 'What do we have to do?'

'You have to try and stop me eating my dinner,' came the reply.

'How do I do that??' asked the younger boy, urging his mind into rapid action.

'You don't have to *really* stop me, just think of things that you could do that *could* stop me.'

'Oh, ok,' said Dan, kind of getting the idea and liking its novelty. Michelle was beginning to show interest in this game that demanded original thinking and innovative approaches. 'Imagine it had pooh on it,' said Danny, weakly.

'That's useless,' said Phil. 'Imagine it's real.'

'I could spit on it!' Dan tried again.

'No, no,' said Phil. 'You have to *do* or *say* something that would really seem to make me not want it.'

'I really *could* spit on it!' the gullible boy suggested.

'Don't be silly,' said Phil, 'that's going too far.'

'Yeah,' volunteered Mitch, 'you may as well offer to pee on it!'
Phil looked at her then back to Danny.

'Come on,' he said. 'You can do better than that.'

Danny was perplexed; it was a good game. It made him think.

'Come on, quick,' said Phil. Martha's footsteps were audible
as they began their descent. Danny was indifferent to the
noise, he was fully concentrating on the game, once she was
down, it would end. Suddenly, an idea rushed in upon him.

'Talk to Mitch for a minute,' he ordered his cousin. Philip was
strangely obedient. While Phil was engaged in some
meaningless exchange of words with his sister, Danny slipped
his hand under the table and reached down to his feet where
as rapidly as he could, he slipped off his right shoe and the
underlying sock. Then, while Phil's gaze was still averted, he
raised his bare foot and planted it firmly on the table
alongside Philip's fork. Phil turned back to view it just as the
kitchen door opened and Martha entered, steaming plate in
hand. Danny's foot was off the table in a flash.

'There you are, Son,' said Martha as she laid the plate down in
front of him.

Philip, the boy who was stuffed himself on chips and fizzy drink, pushed the plate away and getting up, in mock disgust said,

'I cant eat that, Danny just put his stinking foot on the table! I feel sick.' And with that he rushed out and sprinted up to his home.

'That's disgusting!' shouted an incandescent Martha at Danny. And she walked out too. Danny open mouthed was speechless! He looked at his sister who immediately saw through the Machiavellian ploy of her cousin and laughed. Danny got it; how well his cousin had played that game…and him!

~~~~~~~~~~~~~~~~~~~~~~

THE SLAP

It wasn't long before one walking stick was replaced by two as his father's affliction grew steadily worse. Even with that dual support, walking was becoming increasingly difficult and his father only really ventured out of the house now for work, the journey for which had become more challenging than the work itself. Before the first stick had become a permanent feature, he would sometimes take himself to the cinema or take Danny and Michelle to Harringey swimming pool early on a Sunday morning often with JD in tow. Then they would return home and Danny would savour what was for him the best time of the week. The wonderful combination of a bacon sandwich and the Sunday comics, in which a blind Alf Tupper would still be a major threat to his competitors as he ran around that track, trusty guide dog leading the way. The Beano, the Lion and the Hornet as delicious fare as the bacon itself.

That said, even the Sunday morning joy was dependent on Grace's mood. She was, as ever, unpredictable, and as memorable as those mornings were for being the highlight of those Gerrard Road years, they could also be memorable for how unpleasant a taste was left when Grace decided to taint them with one of her warmongering outbursts. Credit to his father on those unsavoury occasions though, as he would cook the bacon in an attempt to preserve the seamless experience of the morning. In fact, this would be the only time he ever saw his father cook.

As well as the pictures and pool and the odd sunday visit to Uncle Bernard's in JD's Renault, the only other place that his father frequented with regularity was the Albert Public House on a Sunday and Monday evening. Even after the initial appearance of the first stick, he would still make the occasional outing to the swimming pool and the pub but these trips became less and less frequent. It was when the second stick made its appearance that his existence became increasingly hermetic with the only excursion into the outside world being his work environment. Even this was no longer performed on the same terms as previously insofar as his father now travelled the two mile trip to Highbury and back by black cab. What expense that must have been. Danny, now 14, often quietly questioned the fiscal prudence of such extravagance and could not see how it was sustainable but assumed that the adults knew what they were doing.

Presumably they must have known what they were doing too when they, Grace and his father, though more his father, slowly increased their consumption of whisky.
This was life now in the basement of Gerrard Road; an emotionally *and* physically crippled man, an emotionally crippled woman and a young boy and girl being prepared for slowly emotionally crippled. When he wasn't working, his father spent most of his evenings in the living room and Grace in the kitchen. They would both revel in their dreams and memories and what could have beens whilst fomenting the fantasy with a fair sprinkling of booze.

There was a formula that emerged over the years, wherein provided the two agents didn't cross paths before around eight o'clock, then there was a strong probability that a war wouldn't erupt that night.

On such nights, Danny could go to bed relatively at ease with the only risk to the calm exterior of the evening being a late night visit from a drunken Grace who would ponificate quietly to the captive audience that was a resting Danny.

He never felt comfortable going to bed leaving his father alone downstairs which presented a conflict between his propensity for early nights and his loyalty to his father who would be alone under the barrage of Grace's poisonous and hostile rants should they erupt.

He had no idea how or what Michelle was thinking all this time although it cannot have been pleasant for her either. It wasn't pleasant for any one of the four of them. However, she still retained that derring do spirit that she had demonstrated with such audacious abandon on a number of occasions previously. Perhaps it was all front, some animalistic attempt to blot out all the immeasurable pain and change that had so altered and influenced her life. But no act of rebellion propelled her to levels of legendary status as much as the time she sneaked out. He couldn't remember the hour exactly but it was night and his father was watching television in the living room with his constant companions, a Player cigarette and tumbler of whisky whilst Grace was alone in the kitchen, smoking her Kensita cigarette (she never inhaled which perhaps explained her greater longevity than her siblings) and hypnotised by the assuaging sounds of *Chanson d'Amour* wafting out of that little portable Philips tape deck.

Danny was just coming out of the toilet which he had almost certainly used for nicotine infusion rather than its primary purpose. As he emerged from its confines, he could just hear the front door opening. At that hour. Who could it be he wondered?

He cautiously mounted the first few steps of the stairs leading to street level where he had waited patiently for hours years before for an aunt's arrival. He could just make out his sister's muffled tones as she whispered to a boy who was at the door. Michelle had discovered boys. It wouldn't be long before Stuart arrived on the scene. Then to his amazement and admiration, he watched as she eased her way out of the door and then, inserting front door key into the lock, gently pulled the door closed behind her, using the key to control the latch so as to ensure no noise sabotaged her plans. He couldnt believe it! What boldness, what risk! How could she be sure that her absence from the house would go unnoticed? It was the same defiance that she had displayed in front of Grace the Elder all over again, she had absolutely no thought nor concern for the consequences.

He was the only person who had been witness to her fearless feat and after he had waited for a few minutes to evaluate the extent of her nerve, he quietly returned to the living room and his father's company passing the audible tones of '*je t'adore*' en route, still stunned by the brazen daring of his older sister. No-one would hear of it from him.

Danny was fifteen and growing; the preceding eight years had stifled the development of his sense of worth as well as impairing his cultivation into a well rounded and confident being. But there was at least one beneficial by product that would ultimately emerge from the whole experience; he would ultimately prove to be astonishingly self-reliant. There were, it seemed, some beneficial side effects from even the most harrowing of upbringings.

It was one of those nights when his father was relaxing in the living room, his aunt in the kitchen and Danny at that table in the kitchen, busy on his homework. By now, study and reading vied for number one spot as his escape outlet.

He could detect the signs of trouble, years of practice had furnished him with reliable prescience born out of entrenched habit. Whenever Grace left the room and entered the living room, there was always the potential threat of rowing and hosilities breaking out. His father never started the rows. This was not a subjectively influenced observation of a biased son so much as observable reality. Grace was the protagonist and often his father would wisely just ignore her ramblings although on occasion, the line was crossed and he would respond, despite Danny urging him to ignore the woman, vocalising this counsel right in front of her.

His father would be more likely to respond to the provocation the more he had imbibed but the arguments were invariably always of the same substance when nothing original was volunteered, just the same accusations, levels of aimed culpability from everything to the wrong shade of eye colour to the crucifixion of Christ himself. It didn't matter, any reason would do.

Whenever she left him and his studies of fifth declension Latin or subject, object, verb order, he would temporarily abandon his education and listen intently to see what tone the conversation next door was taking. That night, it was not an encouraging noise emerging from the living room. Danny was his father's ally and would not leave him alone. He got up and went to join him. Michelle was nowhere in sight.

Maybe she had sneaked out again although there was less need for stealth as she too was older and was less restrained by those totalitarian and rigid dictates that had been for so long devices of suppression in that house.

He sat down on his father's left, between himself and Grace who was standing, intimidating, cursing his father's presence and that of his progeny too. If Danny were ever asked to recite or recount the content of those ravings, he could never recall it precisely as it was so inconsequential and arbitrary. It was the *manner* of their delivery being so caustic and threatening that was and always would be memorable. There was never much swearing nor profanity, in fact Danny never once heard his father use the F word, not once and even the first time Grace used it, it was like a bodyblow, so unused was that kind of language. She used it that night. She was getting more dangerous, like a drug addict who needs stronger and stronger substances or more of the same to receive the same effect.

His father hadn't had that much to drink, he was still able to articulate lucidly and with cogency or perhaps the adrenalin rush negated the effect of the alcohol. Grace was shouting and her cheeks were practically purple with the surfeit of blood flow. This was a mid-terraced house. His father had now given up attempted reason and rather than adopting a complete silent indifference, he was just responding to whatever she said with a curt and abrupt 'Piss off.' The inability to engage him in a belligerent exchange was inflamming her all the more. Danny was still sitting in the chair next to his father, every now and then mouthing to his father a suggestion to ignore her and she would get bored and go away.

After a few minutes of this pointless, asinine, ridiculous venting, his father spoke directly to him.

'I have to go the loo, Dan, just say nothing and I'll be back in a minute.'

'Ok,' said Dan, both males deliberately and overtly ignoring her presence. He watched his father pull himself up on rickety legs, reaching for his walking sticks, one on each side of the armchair, like a gunfighter's guns, ready for instant action. The older man had to turn 180 degrees to facilitate the simple manoeuvre of picking up both sticks, using the arms of the chair as temporary substitutes until the sticks were firmly in his grasp. When he briefly had his eyes on nothing other than the back of the chair, Grace made her move. She was incandescent, outraged that no matter what she said, no matter how she said it, she could elicit no response that would appease her need for hostile offloading. She advanced at pace from the door where she had been standing and as he took the right stick in his right hand, she kicked it away from him and he began to tumble to the floor. Danny was up in an instant, he steadied his father with his left arm and in the same movement swung his right fist in the direction of Grace's face, his father behind him. With a speed that would have graced a leopard and belied his virtual paralysis, he felt the hand of his father as it caught his fist in full flow.

The drama briefly subsided; silence befell the combattants. Grace was breathing heavily, like a pugilist summoning up the blood for a contest but not yet bloodied nor bruised. She left the room, and returned to the kitchen.

'I'm going to the toilet, Danny. Stay here and DO NOT argue with her. Just let her calm down.'

But Danny's spleen now was on fire and rampant too. That woman had just tried to knock his father off his crutches, she had gone too far. When he heard his father finally close the toilet door behind him, he went towards the kitchen with no idea of his intentions. She met him before he entered, in the little hall leading to those four steps. In her grasp was a broom. She hadnt exited thr living room to collect herself or a drink, she had exited to collect a weapon. She lunged at Danny, wielding the broom like some Samurai warrior.

He grabbed the middle of the stick, trying to wrestle it from her but she had the strength of a cornered animal and was surprisingly strong, driven by pent up fury that was overflowing with blistering power. He could not wrest it from her grasp. His father by now had heard the noise and had re-emerged from the toilet. He was slow descending the stairs, but soon she would be one against two, the late 40's woman versus the young adolescent and a crippled man. This was surreal. His father pushed his sons hands away and gripped the broom himself, he was still strong in his arms, and he pulled it aggressively away from the woman who was at bursting point. Danny watched his father as he leaned back against the wall of the hall and attempted to break the cleaning implement over his knee. He couldn't do it, his thighs lacked the strength, the broom was sturdy. He watched as his father, with a peerless innovation and creative thought process, ailing legs notwithstanding, placed the broom under his foot and with a dying strength derived from God knows what source, brought down all the residual force he could muster and snapped the broom in half, throwing the two pieces on the floor with visible contempt. Grace may get away with using verbal assault but she wasn't going to get away with its physical equivalent.

'There,' he cried, 'now let that be enough! Come with me, Danny,' as his father turned to go back into the living room.

'Ok, Dad,' the boy replied, 'in a minute.'

Despite his father's words and actions, it wasn't enough for Grace. She surveyed the remnants of her weapon as his father disappeared into the living room. Still breathing heavily, she placed herself full on and direct in front of Danny and as the boy stared at her, happy that his father had finally stood up to her eternal dominion, he felt the full force of her hand as it slapped him squarely on the cheek. Without thinking, his hand with incipient power delivered the same force to her own cheek causing her to totter backwards, shakingly, visibly shocked that the timid boy, the boy who went to bed early to avoid being late, the boy who tried to stay below the parapet, off the radar, the boy who had had practically every vestige of confidence excised, had finally bared his teeth. There would be no more bullying.

~~~~~~~~~~~~~~~~~~~~

A DANGEROUS AMBITION

It was at the end of the last term of his first year at grammar school that the idea inseminated its seed in his mind. At early morning assembly, the headmaster had scaled the steps of the stage after all other business had been concluded and announced the news that five students had successfully negotiated the rigorous entrance requirements for Oxbridge and that three would be going to Cambridge and two to Oxford. As a reward for such academic achievement, the whole school was to have an additional one day holiday. Without fully understanding the significance of the success itself but recognising its impact, and touched by the influence of a few on the lives of many, even if only one day's worth, Danny decided that in five years time, he too would like to be on that stage, acknowledging the claps of the grateful audience and secure a place to Cambridge. He decided he wanted to go to Cambridge. Not that he had any knowledge of the differences between the two centres of academic elitism, only that the word *Cambridge* sounded more complete, logical and symmetrical. The word *Oxford* to him sounded messy and less structured.

For now the idea sunk to the depths of his conscious imagining and he gave it no further thought. He was a clever boy, of that there was no doubt but he was by no means the *cleverest* boy in his class.

He was in the top stream, the *R* stream, *A* being the middle and *B* the lowest. However, he was never higher than eighth or at a push, seventh amongst his peers.

Children know the status quo; ask any class of any year of any school to rank themselves in the pecking order of practically any genre, and they will do it in a heartbeat. They know who is the toughest, the fattest, the best footballer, the cleverest. It is only adults who seek to muddy the waters of clarity which at grass roots is known to all the participants. And nor do those participants mind; it just is.

The top boy in his class, MB, was just good at every academic subject. Simple as that. And every other kid knew it. They also knew he was useless, quite useless at sport or any other similar activity but in all the academic subjects of the curriculum, he was consistently number one, year after year. The order of rank barely changed over the course of their school careers. Maybe there would be a shift in the proximal position now and then but by and large the order was known, and the teachers knew it too.

Danny didn't particularly like nor dislike school, it was something that had to be done and he was a well behaved and obedient pupil. He still didn't like to place himself on the radar but he did manage to get himself slippered once when he had perpetrated some minor misdemeanour . He remained something of an outsider and was always surprised at lunch times when he would select an empty table to eat his rapidly prepared white roll followed by a penguin biscuit that classmates would join him.

His chess ability was enormously enhanced by attending a lunchtime chess club which was headed by his math's teacher, once more a Polish player of the game but this Pole was very different from the other. This man knew his way around a chessboard.

That man was a truly formidable player and Danny would only ever beat him once in his school career. There was no doubt that Danny was one of the best players that the Pole could call on at lunchtimes to challenge his own splendid talent which explained the more favourable treatment he received in those sternest of mathematical lessons.

He also acquired various swimming medals which activity he had only begun for the facility of shower access. Throughout that time, without those swimming opportunities, for those maturing years of a developing boy, fifteen, sixteen, seventeen and beyond, Danny would have had nothing other than that tin tub as his cleansing device. Nor poor old Michelle whose need for it may have even been greater...

In the meantime, home life was the same. Fights erupting for no clearly definable cause, Grace still begrudgingly tending the culinary needs of all four of the basement dwellers, she fulfilled no other needs, his father becoming less and less mobile, drink becoming more and more apparent and Danny and his sister becoming more and more inured to their uncertain and unstable home life. The boy was quite robust really and was quite a cheery soul, locking away any deep rooted sadness in a dark, distant and unconscious location.

Sometimes however, his sadness leaked out and emerged into the light of his consciousness. One day in his younger years when he was walking out of St John's on the way home, he had been so enthralled in some school activity that he had briefly forgotten, for one solitary and wonderful second, where he was going and all that had happened.

Recollection came rushing in on him like a tidal surge, drowning him in overwhelming sadness and pain and he would never forget as he turned left out of the school gate how he hoped with all his heart that it had all been a dream and he would wake up and he would be in Hampstead and his mum would be alive. But all the self-delusion in the world could not prevent him from knowing he was already awake and that it wasn't a dream at all.

On another occasion, he was at the Vaughan school and he felt the need to talk to someone about his ailing father, his dead mother, his cruel aunt, the awfulness of Gerrard Road, all the rows, all the drink. He didn't expect sympathy from any quarter nor was he seeking it. He was sure there were people worse off than he and maybe the other kids had similar home lives. He didn't want to seem a victim. He had never spoken to anyone about it. Gerrard Road business stayed in Gerrard Road.

Then he spotted the priest; the popular, fluent, Czech born, bald headed priest, the priest who had broken the rules when he divulged secrets to the pupils about sex and the biological imperative. He was a real personality and redoubtable character. And he was a priest. A catholic priest. It was the mid-morning break and Danny was on the outer ring of a small group of boys gathered around the man. There was always a small group of boys around him. He was very popular and with good cause. It was hard not to be drawn to his hypnotic, winsome manner.

Nonetheless, Danny certainly wasn't going to broach the subject of whisky, bad legs and arguments in a public forum like that so he waited for a more opportune moment.

When the priest broke from the group on his way back into the main body of the school, Danny followed and tried introducing the conversation. But it was awkward and he didn't know how best to initiate the topic. He feared he would sound pathetic or self-serving or weak. Furthermore, in his opinion, his manner and bearing didn't reflect that of a child whose nerves were strained at home often to breaking point nor of a child who would frequently apologise to an aunt for something she, not he, had done just in order to re-establish some semblance of fragile peace until the next time.

The only minor indication of something marginally afoot which he didn't consider at the time was his shirt. His shirt was always creased. Never ironed. Even years into his late twenties and on and off even after then, his shirts would remain creased and it wasn't until he read, completely by chance, an article in a magazine in which the Hater of Mondays and the architect of a charity tune that would urge the feeding of the world was quoted as saying when a mother dies leaving a seven year old behind, often one unmissed by product of that event is un-ironed shirts. He viewed Mr G in a much more gentle and sensitive light after reading that article which joined the two entirely different and unconnected men in a bond of communal experience.

Overall then, he was thinking that anything he said would not seem credible and frankly, he wasn't even sure what could be achieved from divulgence of his unhappiness.

'Father,' he began, although the father wasn't giving him much attention. Danny after all, wasn't one of the more popular students and the priest, it had to be said for all his affability, did seem to gravitate more around those students who were more appealing in manner.

'My Dad likes a drink,' he went on. The priest looked around but was clearly not too enthused by the idea of embarking on conversation with this boy. Besides, Danny's words were not conveying any sense of real need nor urgency.

'Erm, yes,' said the priest now conscious of another boy's approach who wanted to discuss something or other but whose approach was much more *normal*. Danny could see he was losing his opportunity. He persevered briefly.

'And then there are quite a lot of rows too,' he said, still half hearted in his delivery. When he thought about it, how *could* Gerrard Road be described to an outsider? It would sound normal, it even suddenly sounded normal to him. The priest was now actively engaged in the alternative discourse and quite uninterested in Danny's further presence. The boy who thought his life was normal added a useful comment about the new subject under discussion simply to cover his retreat and he slipped back into the anonymity of the playground. That would be the last time he ever tried to tell anyone at his school about Gerrard. In fact, it would be years before he would fully tell anyone at all.

He couldn't remember what day it was, nor his precise age but he must have been fifteen given the chronology of the other events and he remembered it was fairly bright in the street since he was sitting downstairs in the kitchen doing homework. Probably late afternoon. Suddenly, some cacophony and turmoil emerged from up at the front door. He ignored it for the moment. He was alone in the kitchen, Grace was upstairs in her room having just got in from work and Michelle was up there too.

The tumult continued and it became impossible to ignore. Danny rushed out and up the four steps, round to the stairs up to the street landing. As he went up two at a time, he could just make out his father on his sticks being assisted in through the front door into the hall by an unknown man, presumably the driver of the black cab that was double parked, engine running. Grace had come out of her bedroom watching and Martha was at the top of the next staircase, seeking to discover the source of the uproar too. Michelle was by her father's other side, helping him in conjunction with the cabbie. 'Oh no,' thought Danny, heavy of heart, 'What now??!'

He continued his rapid climb to the top of the stairs.

'What's wrong?' he said. 'What's going on?' Martha as always wasn't particularly forthcoming. Sometimes it really did seem children in that place were a second rate citizenry.

'Nothing,' she said. 'Your father's not very well.' Really? That was useful. He ignored the totally redundant comment and followed his father who was stumbling into that first room where he slept, supported now just by his sister as the cab driver had returned to his vehicle. He followed the flailing man into the room who dropped heavily onto the bed in a sitting position. Grace was in the room too now, having entered by the partition that separated those two rooms on the ground floor which had originally been one large room. Everybody shared a common sense of disquiet at this uncertain development.

'That's it,' said his father. 'I cant do it anymore?' *Do what?* 'I'm not going back to work, it's too much. I cannot do it anymore,' he continued as he lit a cigarette. Grace said nothing but seemed perturbed and she left the room.

Danny experienced a wave of pure anxiety course through his body. Not his father too, surely not.

'What will you do, Dad?' he said. More disruption, more insecurity, more worry.

'I will give up working.'

'You *cant* give up, Dad!' the boy said, desperate, absolutely not wanting the tears in his eyes to become visible now he was a bigger and older boy. 'You *mustn't* give up, Dad!'

'Don't worry yourself, Dan,' said his father, 'everything will be alright.' But his son wasn't convinced. And he was right not to be convinced. Apart from only a handful of very rare occasions which grew less and less until there were no more, his father never left that living mausoleum again. He didn't die that day but his life practically ended then. And that was not the only ending in that room at that moment. It may take some years yet, but that moment too was the beginning of the end for the experience that was Gerrard Road.

~~~~~~~~~~~~~~~~~~~~~

THE FIRST LETTER

It took some considerable time for the wheelchair to arrive. It was supplied by the NHS and perhaps demand was high or maybe supply low. The delay didn't matter that much because his father hardly ever really needed the wheels. He never went out in the street with it unless to bridge the width of the pavement outside the front door to board a waiting vehicle that would ferry him somewhere on one of those very rare occasions. The journeys in question were either to Bernard's for a Christmas or to Michelle's spousal residence after she had successfully excavated her escape route from that hell hole.

Danny couldn't recall anywhere else his father went. He certainly went nowhere with his son despite repeated pleas a few years later for his father to allow him to wheel him to the Albert so that son and father could have a beer together, trying to inject at least some aspect of normality into this tragic decade of events and into father and son relationship. But no matter how hard he tried, no matter how much he would have loved to have sat in a pub with his dad more than any other person in the world at that point, there was no melting that intractable intransigence. He remembered one spring evening when he was standing just outside the front door with his wheelchair bound father alongside him enjoying the residual beams of the ebbing sun. Danny was employing every resource at his disposal to prevail upon his father to accede to his desperate overtures. The boy was sixteen.

'Come on, Dad!' he pleaded. 'We can be there in five minutes! You can buy me a pint!' No answer.

'I would so love us to have a drink together in the pub, Dad. Pleeeease. Why not? There's nothing to worry about. No one is going to look at you strangely, you don't need to be embarrassed.'

Danny had already begun his drinking career by then but thus far, modestly. Normally.

'Look how lovely an evening it is. And Bob and Mary would *love* to see you after all this time! They really would.' Bob and Mary were the publicans at the Albert and Danny had met them when he had risked getting served underage one Sunday evening. And indeed, they really had asked after their absentee regular.

He was convinced he was making progress, he believed his taciturn father was calculating the risks of allowing himself to be pushed down Gerrard Road on a trip that he had performed countless times in years past and was concluding that there were none. Just as he was hopeful of an *ok let's go* type of response, on the other side of the road turning left from Devonia Road into Gerrard towards them emerged a group of about five or six young men, sixteen years old or so. They were laughing and joking among themselves but it was clearly not laughter directed at Danny's father. They were not even aware of his presence.

'Push me back!' cried the chair bound man.

'Why, Dad? What's the matter?' but Danny knew full well what the matter was; it was that group of boys.

His father was suddenly feeling self-conscious.

Any burgeoning confidence his father was feeling dissolved at once and all lingering hope that his dad and he might pass an hour together in an environment which they had never shared and nor ever would vanished.

'Push me back inside NOW!' repeated his panic stricken father.

'But those boys aren't laughing at you, Dad!'

'I don't care,' said his father. 'PLEASE push me back in.' His father was desperately trying to negotiate the step himself which was preventing his own self-propulsion and he needed his son's assistance.

'Ok, Dad.' And he did his father's bidding.

Once his father was safely transported over the obstacle that impeded his escape exit from self-consciousness, Danny walked out onto the pavement and deliberately preened and postured hoping to attract that group of young men who had no truck with him nor his father but who might have modified their indifference had they heard him call out something offensive which he was sensible enough not to do, as tempted as he was. It wasn't those boys' fault. It was that Danny was bitterly disappointed and needed to point a finger of blame somewhere rather than the only place it could ever be pointed which was arbitrary bad fortune. It was nobody's fault.

For reasons not all clear to Danny, his dad had exchanged bedroom and was now in the back room of the ground floor with Michelle and Grace taking up occupancy in the room next to it, partitioned off from it, nearest to the front door. This is now how it would remain until Michelle finally left home leaving Grace with the entire bedroom. His father's daily routine would now take the shape that it would retain until his end. In the morning, he would awake early, around five am. He would listen to his radio and about six, swing his legs out of the bed, and painstakingly transfer himself to the perfectly positioned wheelchair that would be his residence for the duration of the day until he transferred himself back to his bed between eleven and midnight. After his daughter had left and when Danny was partially gone, he would retire at an earlier hour.

Danny would join him around seven fifteen and keep him company most mornings until eight when he would sprint off down the road to make his purchases. Now there was an added item to his shopping list that so far had comprised just one white roll, the Sun, sometimes, the Daily Telegraph, sometimes both. Not infrequently, when Grace was leaving for work, a fight would erupt, her instigation, and boy and father would sit quietly, dad in the wheelchair, son in the only other chair in the room, at the foot of the single bed, each encouraging the other to ignore the harridan, knowing she had limited time available for her ravings.

They did not always succeed in total non response mode given the provocative and often risible outbursts that would invade their serenity and besmirch their peace.

Even at this point, even when the possibility of fulfillment was fast fading, Danny would occasionally still urge his father to get a flat for the three survivors of Cressy Road. He would say it right in front of Grace when she was engaged in one of her morning diatribes.

'Dad, why don't we get a flat? We still can. Social services could ensure the flat had a slope for your chair, Mitch and me are older now, we could cope and we could leave this dump and this hateful woman to herself.'

'Yes, go!!' screamed Grace, at fever pitch once more, rampant and less restrained with her language now the bubble of non usage had been burst. 'Why don't you just fuck off, and take your sister with you?' His father just raised his finger to his mouth and looked at his son to advocate silence.

The reality was that such a move was impractical; it had been impractical years before because of their youth and now it was impractical again because of their lack of youth. Michelle would not be around much longer and Danny too would flee as soon as he could. That would leave their crippled, dysfunctional father all alone. As loathsome as Grace could be, at least she was company.

His father's existence was barren, his activity minimal. After his son's delivery of the paper in the morning and after he had left for his daily commute, his father would peruse the paper, leave the crossword until last, smoke innumerable cigarettes and watch the limited choice of daytime TV. He particularly liked a programme called Sam. Danny came to like it too although he could only view during holidays. And together they both once watched the whole of the first series of Dallas through one school holiday period.

Despite the barren nature of his life or maybe *because* of it, his father's day was temporally structured to a faultless level of precision. The small bottle of whisky would sit patiently, awaiting its scheduled devourer. He would not pour his first measure until midday and then like clockwork, eke out the remainder over the course of that day until the arrival of Grace would signal a second small bottle. Martha would punctuate his day with periodic visits on her way out for one of her two daily trips to Chapel Market. It was a horribly solitary and unfulfilled life on almost every level imaginable. He had a medical latrine for his personal needs and his dinner, still a Grace creation, would be served to him in that small tomb like room. It was horrible.

This was his existence, day after day, night after night. Sometimes, Bernard would pop in to spend some time with his brother but such days, as welcome as they were for breaking up the inexorable monotony of a life spent, had deleterious side effects. The unexpected visits entailed unexpected whisky. The genie of overindulgence slipped its bottle. Bernard would eventually depart, off to re-embrace the blanket of his loving home environment, his brother would remain to re-embrace the emptiness of his life.
Danny, conscious of the level of smoking and drinking that was integral to his father's routine used to ask him to promise not to die from a heart attack.

'Don't be so silly,' his father would say. 'Quit worrying, why on earth are you thinking about heart attacks at your age?' A long familiarity with illness was why. 'I'm fine.' Actually, he wasn't fine at all, self-delusional was more accurately descriptive.

It was decision time at school; Danny was now coming to the end of his fifth year, year eleven in contemporary terms. He had to choose which were to be his A-level subjects in the sixth form. Naturally, there was no parental guidance, no familial suggestions at all. He didn't mind that, he was increasingly used to relying on his own resources and decision making faculties. He excelled at ancient languages, English and history and although he really enjoyed physics and maths, he just wasn't very good at them. His French was more than acceptable but didn't stand out.

Unfortunately, the combinations of subjects available could not be dissected and re-amalgamated. When the form master asked the class who intended to take Latin, Ancient Greek and Ancient History, the set of A-levels which took place in the red bricked building across the road, the home of the first to third years, no-one raised their hand. A-level choice decision was a pivotal turning point as options narrowed thereafter. Danny allowed pragmatism to resolve the conflict. Better to be a big fish in a small pool he thought, than a shrimp in a sea of whales. He slowly raised his hand. Three more hands followed his. The die was cast.

It was early on in his first year of sixth form that the ambition of five years earlier suddenly returned with vigour and possibility. Their two rotating teachers advised them that any of the four that wanted to attempt the Oxbridge entrance exam would be allowed to do so. All four volunteered for the task, three of them electing Cambridge, one opting for Oxford.

The options lacked any ambivalence. Sitting and passing that most punishing and gruelling of exams before A-level (this route was called fourth term as the exam was taken in the fourth term of sixth form) would mean a requirement only to attain two E's at A-level to matriculate, the idea behind this concept being that the level required to pass the entrance was so high, especially at that young age, that it would dwarf the A-level standard. The other option (seventh term, that is the term after the completion of sixth form's normal six terms) was to sit the A-levels before the entrance exam, seeking to attain the highest grades possible and then hoping that those results, combined with the interview, would be sufficient to secure entry if the entrance exam result was not outstanding. This latter option would clearly involve an additional year at school following completion of the normal two year sixth form.

What made the entrance exam so testing was its lack of a pass mark. Student was competing against student, from all corners of the globe. It was gladiatorial, brutal and demanded the highest application. There was no point in aiming for anything other than perfection in that exam. In short, it was ruthless; the more popular the subject, the harder it was to succeed, with some disciplines, such as maths, being subject to competition of at least fifteen applicants for every place available.

Danny saw the second option as a redundant and wasteful use of time and his background had caused him to develop a belief that time shouldn't be used profligately as fate can upset the most modest of plans and intentions.

He elected the pre A-level route when he would be seventeen, not more than ten months away. At least if he failed, he would not have wasted a year that could be spent productively in some other activity. The other three decided upon the same course. The workload was unforgiving. These boys had to attain greater proficiency than A-level and beyond more than a year before A-levels had to be taken. And then there was the general paper. This had no formal revision protocol nor precedent. The only preparation for that paper was reading all the leading articles of all the broadsheet newspapers practically everyday. How boring it seemed and yet what breadth of knowledge these young minds were assimilating without being fully aware of their increasing strength of mind.

At home in the evenings, Danny spent more and more time in the kitchen studying, honing his skills, reading about subjects in the Times and Telegraph and Guardian that seemed so irrelevant to his life and yet opened worlds he had never previously considered. The Latin and Greek he was translating and improving was so much harder than what now seemed like the pedestrian material he had been used to. He was outgrowing Gerrard Road and Grace who seemed smaller and smaller as she still tried to cling onto her earlier power over the little boy that he used to be. She would still frequent the kitchen when he was intent on his studious travail, and after a few beakers of whisky or a Guinness or two would remind him how he was nothing and that he would never be able to compete with the might of her cerebral prowess.

She wasn't worth even his minimum attention anymore. He had never been more focused and actually, he would never be as focused again in his life.

He really wanted this, he wanted to get into Cambridge from the bottom of his heart. He wasn't even familiar with the machinations and the real meaning of the place but he knew it represented a universe of difference from his wretched and miserable life. All his years at the Vaughan, he had looked up at the Honours Board which adorned the wall opposite the staff room in the new building. Inscribed into this testimony of achievement were all the alumni who had successfully attained Oxbridge or St Bartholomew's. His cousin Martin's name was among the eulogized for his entry to Barts and a medical career which would witness his ascent to high office.

He had always gone to bed early since his arrival in Islington and he had come to love the early morning and always would. Perhaps it was the potential of a brand newness that a new day signified, perhaps he disliked the night as it represented the death of that day's hope and potential. In that intense study period, he would rise at 6 am, when the house would be swamped with peace, no Grace, no friction. He would descend to the kitchen, put the kettle on and ready himself for a couple of hours study before school. His father's bedroom was immediately above the kitchen and Danny knew that his dad would be awake and he would make a cup of tea for his dad too, and transport it upstairs for him.

'Thanks, Dan,' he would say quietly as he lay there, cigarette already aglow, contemplating the sameness of the day that was ready to unfurl like the day before and every other day for countless numbers previous.

'Would you like me to sit with you, Dad?' the boy would ask.

'No!!!' said his father. 'You go and study! I'm fine, honestly. You go and study.'

'Ok.' But as he re-traced his steps downstairs, he knew he wouldn't go and study. He wouldn't be able to concentrate knowing his lonely father was above him, with nothing to do, with no-one to talk to and he would simply collect his own tea and go back up and then sit with his father until it was time to get the paper. He didn't really mind. It was his dad and no matter what, he loved his dad. He would never regret sacrificing that revision time to keep his father company.

The exam was approaching; the work was intensifying as realisation that the hour was practically upon them. The four boys who had become close in that small classroom that had housed them in its inner sanctum and who had shared the same ambition, discussed what they would do if they failed. One of them, the one with whom Danny had most in common, though they probably would not have been friends had circumstances not dictated events, was clear that he would not go to any other university if he failed to make this, his first choice. The other two were less rigid and displayed a more stoical approach stating that they would go to another university in which they would excel given all this preparation. The fact that one of those two was MB, the boy who had consistently and constantly been the best in the class year after year, meant that his view was not really relevant since the likelihood of him failing to gain access to Oxford was beyond the realms of remoteness. Danny knew for sure what he would do. He had set his heart on Cambridge, although the specific reasons for such insistency were unknown to him. If he failed to get in, he would leave school and get a job, maybe on the London Underground like his father before him, like his sister. He was investing everything into Cambridge however; for him, this was the fight of his life.

Cambridge and Oxford are made up of various colleges; it isn't one amorphous entity like red brick equivalents. Cambridge and Oxford are the umbrellas and the colleges are their ribs. Each has its own identity, own colours, own scarf and there even exist rivalries between the various fraternities. When making the selection, three colleges had to be nominated in preferential order. Most hopeful applicants would have only a glossy prospectus from each as their guide as there was little point in visiting the establishment before even being accepted. Besides, many of those seeking entry lived too far away to merit the trip. Danny wasn't sure why he picked King's College as his first choice, it may have been because of its wide acclaim and more recognisable to the general public than some of the more unfamiliar names which were nonetheless bona fide Cambridge components

Once the exam had been taken, no letter was forthcoming with a grade or a statement of pass or fail; notification that you had satisfied the academic requirement was by way of a request for interview from the nominated college. The exam alone, as arduous as it was, was not enough, it was simply the key to the door to the interview. The interview would be more a device wherein the compatibility, the potential harmonious symbiosis of the student and college could be evaluated. It was conducted on a one-to-one basis with the student facing what would be his or her head of studies in the subject elected for education should they succeed in being accepted. There was some academic inquiry in the interview but that was not its principle purpose, the academic excellence had already been demonstrated with the punishing papers previously sat; the interview was more about personality.

The first day of a series of days arrived; there were a number of exams testing the student in the various disciplines he sought to study as well as the unpredictable general paper. Each paper was three hours long and unlike every other exam Danny ever sat, he didn't finish early. Every second, every minute was spent in total concentration and effort. He would *never* in his life sit exams as difficult as those proved to be. After each gargantuan effort, he left the examination hall drained but could not afford to let up or relax until the entire set had been completed. The accompanying stress took its toll too. However, the upside for that young man, outweighed the potential personal catastrophe of failure. The risk was worth it.

The exams finally came to an end. Now the waiting, the anxious and detestable waiting. Gerrard Road was quiet or more likely, Danny was so engrossed in his crusade that he was oblivious to any outbursts to which he was by now largely inured. It was late 1978. James Callaghan was Labour prime minister but Margaret Thatcher would not have to wait too much longer before she took the reins of political power that would alter the face of politics for decades to come, Viv Anderson was England's first black footballer player and Danny was awaiting what may be the finest Christmas present he had ever received. The letter arrived one November morning. He was still in the habit of rising early, although now, when he passed the time with his father, there was no reason to feel trickles of guilt that he was not studying in the kitchen below. The postman's arrival was no longer the indifferent event that it had been to date. It now proffered promise, hope as well as potentially unspeakable disappointment. As to be expected, in those days he was the first at the door when the letter box issued its metal alert.

That day was no different. As the clock approached the habitual hour when the postman executed his duty, Danny would stand up, turn the TV's volume down and move closer to the door, listening for any warning in advance of the metal snapping and the light fall of enveloped paper to earth. There it was; as always, he was there in seconds, seeking his name emblazoning the envelope and a postcode that would definitively identify the origins of the missive. CB was all he needed to see. And that morning he did see it. There was some other post of no interest to him at all and he walked back with envelope in hand into his father's bedroom and sat down, calmly and quietly.

'Well?' said his father, removing a Player from its pack, 'Is that it?'

'It must be,' said his son not even considering that his father for all his introspection, all the ineffable misery that drowned him daily, was almost certainly as desperate for his son to receive good news as his son himself.

'Well, aren't you going to open it?' said his dad, drawing heavily on the white paper cylinder in his mouth.

'Yes, I am,' he confirmed 'but I just want to enjoy these last moments of peace in case it's not offering me an interview.'

'Ok,' said his father, wisely and sensitively saying no more, leaving his son to his own thoughts despite aching to know the contents himself. After a minute or so, the crippled man spoke again. 'Shall I open it for you?' Danny looked up and considered the offer.

It sounded like a good offer. He started to extend his hand towards his father, clasping the small white envelop, not A4, not even A5 size, did that mean anything he wondered, then snatched his hand back.

'No thanks, Dad, I'll do it.' And with that he inserted his index finger into the top corner of the envelope and drew it back exposing the entrails to the world. He removed the folded letter inside and indifferently discarded the empty shell remaining. He was partially aware of his father's gaze on him as he unfolded the carefully layered pleats of the paper extending it into its full A4 stature and read the contents. His father moved his eyes to the muted screen of the television, changing shapes with no vocal collaboration but he wasn't really watching it. It lacked even less appeal that morning than normal.

Danny lowered his hand that held the paper loosely and looked at the wall before him. Then he raised the paper again and read the words once more. This boy who could translate Euripides from the original Ancient Greek, who could recite Virgil in Latin and could compose his own lyrical verse in those dead languages was struggling with basic English prose.

'Well?' said his father now understandably impatient. Danny, impassive, expressionless, began to read.

"Dear Mr O'Leary, following appraisal of your application to King's College, Cambridge and the concomitant exam results, we would like to invite you for further assessment and interview at King's College on Monday the 11th of December at 11.15 am. Please see below for details of time, location and requirements for the day. Thank you for your interest in our institution. Yours sincerely…etc…". A big breath.

'I've got an interview, Dad!!' he screamed. 'I've got an interview!!! I have GOT an interview!!!' and he jumped up, ran over to his dad and gave him a kiss and a hug and then crumpled the letter in clasped hands as he looked up to ceiling and repeated quietly to himself, 'I've got an interview!!!'

'Well done, Danny boy!' said his father, 'well done!'

~~~~~~~~~~~~~~~~~~~~~

THE INTERVIEW

Stuart, his sister's boyfriend lent him a suit for the occasion but never asked for it back. It was one of those thick material concoctions, insipid fawn colour with flared trousers to finish off the quite heinous looking thing. But it was a fashionable item at the time and when Danny turned out of Gerrard on the way to the Angel station, even his shirt was ironed thanks to the insistence of his sister who did the pressing herself. He went to Cambridge unaccompanied and nervous knowing what was at stake. He had never travelled this far alone but it was relatively straightforward and the directions in the letter were laid out in a comprehensible and clear manner. He arrived in good time, found the college and the room where the interview was to take place and once conversant with the location to ensure no late arrival, he wandered around the imposing grounds of the college.

Finally, the hour of the interview arrived and he knocked nervously at the door. A young man, long, tangled and bedraggled dark hair, stubble protruding from his chin opened the door. He was wearing old blue corduroy trousers with a baggy jumper out of shape which was hanging limply over the top. He was wearing no shoes. The man looked comfortable, dressed at ease, quite differently from the way Danny felt and must have looked. The room itself was beautiful and archaic, sloping ceiling, oak panelled walls and an aura of warmth and seclusion pervaded its interior. The man sat on a divan type affair inviting Danny to take a chair opposite him which, once sitting, gave Danny greater height and prominence than the man who was practically sprawled before him.

From the outset, it didn't go well. The boy was overdressed but not even elegantly so and his clothing stunted and stilted him. The man asked questions about politics, left wing substance predominantly and Danny answered fairly knowledgably but without bias as his political proclivity was undetermined and indistinct. Not a great deal of time was spent on the subject matter of his intended pursuit nor aspects of life at the college itself. The meeting lacked enthusiasm and animation. He was aware that he was presenting a wooden image lacking anything other than two dimensional substance. By the time the interview was drawing to a close and the stubbled man was inviting questions, Danny just wanted to return to London, to the hovel he was seeking to escape. If this was salvation, he would rather remain where he was. However, that he was there at all meant his academic results had been powerful. He wasn't rejected yet…

~~~~~~~~~~~~~~~~~~~~~~~~

THE SECOND LETTER

The time scale was known to all; the decision would be made and the confirmation letters would be sent out before Christmas. Once more, he sat with his father awaiting the postman's delivery. He had discussed the content of the interview and its bearing with his father over and over. It wasn't so much a discussion as a monologue wherein Danny would seek to re-interpret every word he could recall, evaluating every nuance. His father patiently sat quiet, smoking and allowing his son to use him as a sounding board. The man knew that it was now out of their hands. The talking for his son served as a useful distraction in those early mornings to help while away the time.

The day the second letter arrived, CB postmark evident and the day the same ritual was observed, the collection of the missive and the withdrawal to the room where his father was practically held captive by his paralysis of body and mind, Danny once more read silently before airing the content aloud. He didn't get far before the suffocating sensation of all the wasted effort and the choking effect of his tears stopped him as he softly read out loud,

'We thank you for your time and effort but regret to inform you…' There was no jumping up and down for joy this time, no celebration of hope fulfilled, just a young boy in an armchair exhausted with the effort of his mental exertions that had meant so much to him, with a cigarette smoking father not more than a metre away not knowing what he could say to ease his son's heartbreak. Father and son sat silent, equally bathed in disappointment.

~~~~~~~~~~~~~~~~~~~

THE END OF THE FIRST CHAPTER

When applying for Cambridge in those days and almost certainly still the same procedure today, three colleges would be nominated by the hopeful academic. The fact was all the colleges were and are very similar academically, the only significant differences being that some colleges were recognised as stronger and more universally noted for certain disciplines, for example, at the time Trinity College was a powerhouse for mathematics. And academic subjects, although Cambridge was predominantly an academic institution above all else, were not the only strength for which some colleges were renowned, Fitzwilliam being the prime example of this as being the magnet for top class rugby players and other sportsmen. It did appear that if the student's first choice proved unsuccessful, then the second and third options never seemed to open their doors to that individual, almost as though out of spite for not being first preference. Although this is speculation rather than accepted fact.

The rejected students were placed into the *pool* as it was known. Essentially, all those colleges who had rejected their first batch of applicants would now have the opportunity to look at all those students who had themselves been rejected by their first choices.

Ironically, although on the face of it this may seem to offer more possibility of entry than the primary route, it was actually much more difficult since all those pool entrants were competing against many more of similar academic pedigree than just against those who had also applied for the same first choice college.

It should be remember that *all* the students who had managed to progress to the interview stage had passed the pre-requisite academic levels. The pooled student would have no idea which college if any would pick them and even if they did, this would simply be the door opening to interview stage once more.

However, the pool obviously meant there was still hope, still possibility of entry to one of the finest universities in the world even though the odds of success were now quite poor. Of Danny's class, MB had, as expected, secured his first option at Oxford, and one of the other lads had been accepted at Magdalen, a very religious outlet at Cambridge. That student would one day attain relatively high status in the Catholic church. Danny and the boy with whom he had the most in common were the two who had been placed in the pool.

After the initial wave of unimaginable disappointment that winter morning, Danny had recovered to some degree and hope was struggling to oust pessimism as his principle sentiment. After a joyless Christmas, even more joyless than the usual Gerrard Christmases could be, Danny returned to school in January 1979, impatient but not quite as dejected as the previous December. His two teachers were upbeat and trying to sound positive in an attempt to fortify the spirits of the two downcast young men. The disappointment of their failure did to a large extent undermine the unbridled joy of the two who had savoured success but to the credit of those two Oxbridge students in waiting, they subdued any ostentatious manifestation of delight out of support for their fellow examination warriors. Their revelry in their own achievements would remain in check until the final outcome of the pool was known.

There was at least the knowledge that there was a final date by which the results of that pool had to be disclosed, and that was the end of January. If no letter had arrived by the end of that month, they would know they were out of the game.

In the meantime, there were now A-levels to be addressed which would be sat in May-June of that year. Frankly, the standard which all those four boys had attained by the preparation for the gruelling entrance exam had elevated them to levels so far above the standards demanded by A-level that it would be like a racing car driver being told he had to take a test in a Noddy car. Danny practically stopped all academic work. None of the teachers at school much cared now. These boys had proved their academic mettle, they had been scarred in a war of erudition, they had earned their spurs and their right of passage in sweat, toil and ambition. He began frequenting the pub more. He began to read all those books that study of such high brow literature had prevented him from so doing. He devoured Hemingway's *Old Man and the Sea,* tears brought on at the end by the old man's unrewarded and unbelieved efforts, he guzzled up *For Whom the Bells Toll* by the same author and was delighted when the film was shown on the television with Gary Cooper and Ingrid Bergman bringing those wonderful central characters to life. He seemed to gravitate towards heroic endings tinged with pathos.

But all the while, all he did, all he read, all he watched was underpinned by a quiet resignation, a stoical calm, a lingering hope, awaiting the outcome and decisions being made by those anonymous titans of academia.

He was silently praying for a letter adorned by CB at the top right of the envelope in which he was invited for interview once more but this time he knew as grateful as he would be for that, it would only be the interview and not an offer of a place.

Every evening he would carry himself home as the nights drew in, the cold and damp infiltrating his every pore, the winter wind finding his coat no obstacle for its heartlessly piercing penetration. Every dark evening as he traipsed along Colebrook Row by himself as he left the Angel station on the walk back to Gerrard, he would feel the sense of anticipation rise as the house got nearer. There was no Philly anymore, although he would still play *BB* himself, mentally explaining to the imaginary audience that Fred Smith had retired now but that Erebus would continue to fly the flag alone. He still sped past unsuspecting pedestrians who had no possible idea that they were Ethiopian or French or American or any other national athletes, just overtaken by the ineluctable British Boy.

He would turn into his street, when for the next two minutes, he was filled with unlimited hope and expectation, arriving home, turning his key in the lock, looking straight at the table that abutted from the wall in the hall where post was placed for its various recipients' collection to see if there was anything on it. Sometimes there was but not for him.

Hope for that day expunged, he would walk heavily down to the living room where would be sitting his sister and his father who still managed to walk one flight of stairs for the purposes of exercise and resistance to total and final paralysis.

There he would sit for a while, with his father and his sister, until he decided or could summon the interest to change out of his school clothes. He was dreaming his own impossible dream.

Midway through January, the other pooled boy received a letter from Pembroke College. He had an interview. When he broke the news to his three colleagues before lessons had begun, the three, including Danny were delighted for him. There was genuinely no enmity nor rivalry between those four. They did not feel that they were competitors even though the two pooled boys had inadvertently become such. They wanted each other to do well. That intense period of those lives, that overwhelming exam preparation, those after school classes, that common purpose, these things combined to create a powerful bond between them. They were not natural friends and would not remain in contact but for that brief period they truly were a small band of brothers.

Danny was now the only one who had heard nothing. It wasn't his lack of ability, he had clearly demonstrated his mental agility. His lack of interpersonal skills, being socially cumbersome, his evident ineptitude when trying to make small talk, his woeful sense of sartorial smartness were the elements that afforded him no favours. But there was still time. And every night he would perform the same ritual, sit increasingly downhearted down in the living room. Having to endure another twenty four hours before that rising of hope would re-surface as he turned into Gerrard Road. Every morning, his fellow scholars would ask if he had heard anything as if he wouldn't have volunteered that information without prompting.

Time was running out; it was fast approaching the end of January. The nights were dark and so was he. His hope was fading more and more and his sense of expectation upon entering the house was discernibly less. One January night that seemed to be the same as every other January night, he went through the same motions. Down Gerrard Road he traipsed, hoping, praying. He opened the front door, pushing it shut as he looked at the table. There was one letter on it; not overly optimistic, he picked it up and looked at the addressee. It was for Grace. He walked downstairs and entered the living room where Michelle was slumped in an armchair and his father in another, the one when Grace had once sought to knock him off his sticks. They were both smoking their respective brands. His father had a small quantity of whisky in his glass, almost certainly not the first but he didn't seem drunk. Danny dropped down onto the settee in a heap, stripped of all vitality.

'No post again,' he announced to the room but not really interested in his own words nor who heard them.

'No,' said his dad 'but..'.

His son gave him no chance to finish. Suddenly his energy replenished itself and he leapt to his feet.

'But? BUT? BUT WHAT, Dad?? Tell me!!'

'Give me a chance!' said his father, sitting upright as best he could and with shaky hands, reaching for a piece of paper that he had deposited beneath his glass. 'You have had a phone call.'

'What phone call?' entreated his son, barely able to contain himself. 'Who from? Tell me, tell me!' His dad passed him the piece of paper as he spoke.

'Three colleges called. I've put their phone numbers on the paper, and the names, there was Jesus, Queens' and I think Corpus Christi. They are written there. They wanted to know if you could go for interview.'

'Which one?' said Danny, slightly confused at being used to no news at all to suddenly receiving so much of it.

'All of them,' said his dad. 'I said you would call them tomorrow to arrange a time.'

'All of them?' he said looking intensely at his father. 'You are telling me that these three colleges' -he looked down again at the piece paper just to make sure he wasn't misreading- 'have phoned today asking me to call and arrange an interview?'

'Yes, Danny. For god's sake, calm down!' But Danny couldn't calm down, he was beside himself, he rushed into the kitchen where the phone was located and although it was after five thirty, he called one of the numbers. There was no reply. He was terrified if he didn't phone immediately they would retract their offer. He wanted to phone his school, his headmaster, perhaps the head could do something now but of course, it was too late for that too. He would have to be patient until the morning. Besides, as he calmed down, he thought about it. He had three interviews with three colleges. THREE! There was still hope! There was *still* a chance! THERE WAS STILL HOPE…..

~~~~~~~~~~~~~~~~~

6876646R00116

Printed in Great Britain
by Amazon.co.uk, Ltd.,
Marston Gate.